# Mel Bay Presents
# Mandolin
## Crosspicking Technique

### By
### Mickey Cochran

Copyright ®1997 by Mickey Cochran
Published by Mel Bay Publications
Visit us on the Web at http://www.melbay.com — E-mail us at email@melbay.com

# Table of Contents

# Table of Contents

# The Crosspicking Mandolin Technique Book

## Introduction

Crosspicking mandolin has immense roots. A culmination of many styles, artists, and instruments inspires the technique of crosspicking. Because the mandolin itself dates back many centuries, as a member of the lute family, approaches to playing the mandolin have been myriad and varied. Usually the style of music would dictate the approach. As to crosspicking, many styles of music can be effectively played so that crosspicking itself dictates the style. An example of this is to take a simple classical melody like "Greensleeves" and adapt it to a banjoistic roll (crosspicking) on the mandolin; suddenly, the piece takes on a Bluegrass feel and becomes difficult to categorize.

The mandolin has usually been categorized as an ensemble instrument.* Many times a mandolinist will grapple when asked to play a piece unaccompanied. In spite of its capability as a lead instrument, the mandolin has always been underrated as a solo instrument—excluding certain classical mandolin pieces. With applied crosspicking technique, the mandolin becomes a forceful solo instrument capable of filling a room with colorfully supported melodies. Crosspicking bombards the listener with a barrage of notes. As is similar to Bluegrass banjo, crosspicking mandolin doesn't seem to pause for a breather. A continuous succession of notes pours forth establishing the melody while filling in all of the spaces with harmony notes. Not only does the mandolin support itself, with spaces filled harmonically, but crosspicking technique works effectively for supporting other lead instruments and vocals. As an accomplished mandolin player, you are or would be capable of varying the backup of an ensemble (band) with many colorful approaches; for example, one verse you may want to add tremolo† backup while the second verse you could apply a crosspicking backup.

The mandolin has mostly been associated with country and bluegrass. Today, it has transgressed rock, jazz, and new age music. No matter what style of music you enjoy playing, learning the many applicable possibilities of crosspicking will enhance your musical creativity. There are no limitations on how or where crosspicking can be applied. It's truly one approach to the mandolin that can be adapted to any style of music.

This is a methodology book designed for the intermediate to advanced mandolinist. It will offer you, as a mandolin player, a new voice. Or, if you're already crosspicking, many new ideas can be added to your arsenal. Each song includes a preparatory study that allows you the opportunity to gain a solid footing before attempting the piece itself. These studies can be applied in other areas as backup ideas, song ideas or takeoffs for improvisation. So, don't think of them only as exercises. Be creative and experimental.

This book was musically written in tablature (a number system)—you will not have to know, or learn, how to read music. If you know how to count, you can read tablature—just start from the beginning and pay careful attention to instructions and what each tab symbol indicates. All of the songs start with simple preparatory exercises that summarize any difficult passages; by accomplishing these exercises thoroughly, the songs will easily follow. Don't get impatient with your progress; remind yourself that you're playing the mandolin because it's fun!

* An instrument that is usually accompanied by other instruments.
† A rapid down-and-up stroke simulating a continuous tone.

# Part I: Mandolin & Crosspicking Basics

## Getting Oriented

How do you focus on a new technique and bypass the normal frustration involved with learning new habits and maybe even shedding old ones to accomplish the task? There are many approaches to playing the mandolin; many of them haven't even been invented yet! The more you can learn about your chosen instrument, the closer you come to actualizing your musical goals. Whether you play the mandolin as an accompanist or instrumentalist, your arsenal of licks, chords and techniques is what you depend on. If you haven't already, once you've incorporated crosspicking into your arsenal, you'll wonder how you've played so long without this colorful texture.

To become oriented in the task of learning crosspicking involves setting short-time goals. Become familiar with the foundation and build your skills with each exercise in the order they are taught. Reward yourself with the sense of accomplishment that follows after mastering a crosspicking exercise or arrangement. And, don't let anybody tell you that crosspicking is easy. There are times when you will hit the wall and feel like you're not getting anywhere fast. Your best strategy in this case is to go back over what you've learned up to this point and keep on practicing. Before long, you'll find yourself smoothly moving forward to other goals.

*Enjoy The Journey*

## Practice Makes Perfect

Well we've all heard that maxim one too many times! Even so, the truism lives on. You cannot move from "a to b" without practicing. No one starts from the top of the mountain; some of us just climb faster than others.

### Step 1: Set up a practice schedule.

The consequence: you'll see very little progress in accomplishing your goals. Keep a journal of what, when, and how much you practiced. Set up small goals to accomplish and notate your progress as you go along.

### Step 2: Carry a road map.

If you want to reach the summit quickly, carry a road map. You need a guide to assist you in developing habits or technique to make accomplishing the task easier and more efficient. This book is one of many. Research your interests and start a library of instructional material that you can glean new songs and technique from.

### Step 3: Make sure your tools are sufficient.

Your mandolin does not necessarily have to be an expensive instrument to learn on. Although, if it's not set up properly, you'll become frustrated trying to accomplish any musical goals with it. For instance, if the instrument has a high action (strings being abnormally high off the fretboard), you will not be able to comfortably fret the notes making it impossible to crosspick with ease. If the bridge is not properly located, your intonation (tuning) will be off making it difficult to tune your mandolin. If you haven't up to now, I'd highly recommend taking your mandolin to a luthier (instrument specialist) for proper setup.

# Tuning, Strings & Things

## Tuning Preparation

Ease of tuning your mandolin is determined by many factors:

**1. Intonation:** If your bridge is not properly placed on the body, your mandolin will become next to impossible to tune. To test whether your bridge is properly placed or not, try playing 12th fret harmonics on each string followed by fretting at the 12th fret. If the pitch does not match on any of the strings, then the bridge is not properly placed for intonation. One string may be closer than others indicating that the bridge is very close to where it should be, but the individual strings aren't properly compensated. In either case, I recommend that you take your mandolin to a luthier for proper setup.

**2. Strings:** If your strings are old, replace them. Strings become corroded and nicked over time making them very difficult to tune properly. If your strings are not properly weaved through the eye of your tuning keys, you may have slippage causing the instrument to be constantly going out of tune. Consult with a luthier or music store on how to properly replace your strings.

**3. Frets:** Worn frets can cause many intonation problems. Usually fret wear occurs at the first five frets of your instrument. Look closely for grooves directly under where your strings are fretted to determine if you may have this problem. If so, have a luthier replace or file them as may be required.

**4. Keys:** Tuning keys do wear out! The gears can be damaged causing the revolutions to vary.

**5. Nut:** Many times a string can get caught in the process of tuning it within the groove of the nut. To remedy this, try placing a small amount of graphite within the groove. If this doesn't correct the problem, you'll have to take it in to a luthier for replacement or repair.

## String Gauges

The string gauge will influence playability of your mandolin greatly. Crosspicking is such a demanding technique for stretches and chording that it is critical to use either light or medium gauge strings. Heavy gauge strings would not be recommended for crosspicking due to their weightiness. I use medium gauge since there's a sacrifice in volume when using light gauge. Although, if you're just starting out, or have never attempted crosspicking before, I recommend light gauge strings. If you want, upon accomplishing the technique of crosspicking, you can graduate to medium gauge strings. Light gauge strings are definitely easier to fret, you'll find yourself not fighting with the instrument as much as you would with medium gauge strings.

Strings also come in many alloys. Crosspicking sounds great on bright, brassy strings. Try a phosphor bronze alloy if you like this characteristic. Otherwise, if you prefer a more mellow tone, try nickel wound strings. As there are so many stylists, there are also many different tastes in strings. The choice usually reflects the artist's taste and will usually become a signature of that particular artist. Experiment and discover what works best for you.

To keep your strings sounding bright and easy to tune, clean them often. Consult with your local music store for what products work best for this purpose.

# Tuning Methodology

## Methods of Tuning

The mandolin is tuned exactly the same as a violin; the only difference is the mandolin has a chorus of two strings tuned in unison for each note. From the 4th string (G), each string is tuned a fifth above: G - D - A - E. There are many approaches that can be utilized effectively for tuning your mandolin. The important thing is to know at least two approaches so that you can verify that it's tuned properly with a second approach. Before we learn these approaches, you'll need a starting reference for one of the strings. The best tool to have at your disposal is a tuning fork that vibrates at 440 Cycles equaling "A". This is the same pitch as the 2nd string from the bottom on your mandolin. After matching up the tuning fork with your "A" strings, you're prepared to utilizing the following tuning methods.

### Tuning Method 1

**Step 1:** Place your fourth finger (little finger) on the 7th fret of the "A" strings (2nd strings)—This note is "E" and should match your 1st strings. Tune one of your first strings until the pitch matches. Follow with tuning the "E" strings in unison with each other.

**Step 2:** Place your fourth finger on the 7th fret of the "D" strings (3rd strings)—This note is "A" and should match your 2nd strings. Tune the "D" string until it matches your "A" strings.

**Step 3:** Place your fourth finger on the 7th fret of the "G" strings (4th strings)—This note is "D" and should match your 3rd strings. Tune the "G" string until it matches your "D" strings.

Upon completing this first tuning method, you're now ready to verify if it's correct by utilizing a second tuning method.

### Tuning Method 2

This method requires the ability to play "harmonics". Instructions for learning to play harmonics are in the sidebar of this page.

**Step 1:** Play a harmonic above the 12th fret of the "A" strings. This pitch should match the 1st strings fretted at the 5th fret. If it doesn't, attempt to fine tune the 1st string before moving on to Step 2.

**Step 2:** Play a harmonic above the 12th fret of the "D" strings. This pitch should match the 2nd strings fretted at the 5th fret. If it doesn't, attempt to fine tune the 2nd strings before moving on to Step 3.

**Step 3:** Play a harmonic above the 12th fret of the "G" strings. This pitch should match the 3rd strings fretted at the 5th fret. If it doesn't, attempt to fine tune the 3rd strings.

Now that you've verified how close you came with the Tuning Method 1, try going back to it to see if it is tuned consistently. If not, your intonation may be considerably off, or you still may need practice at tuning. Developing an ear to determine pitch can be accomplished by listening carefully and always referencing where you're at by fretting notes above and below the note being tuned. Experiment and take your time.

### How to Play Harmonics

*Natural harmonics occur at the 5th, 7th, and 12th frets of your mandolin. This division also repeats past the 12th fret. By placing your finger lightly above any string above these particular frets while striking the string with your pick, you'll hear a bell-like tone ring out. If not, keep experimenting by touching the string simultaneously as you pick it. Notice that by lifting the finger slightly, directly after picking the note, you will create a louder bell tone.*

# Mandolin Tablature Staff & Numbers

Tablature is one of the oldest forms of notating music. It's a number system that follows a simple logic for mandolin: each number represents the fret distance and each line represents a pair of strings. Of course, other considerations include timing and embellishments. Please pay careful attention to the following tablature indications and refer back to them whenever necessary.

## The Staff

*The staff consists of 4 lines each representing a string on the mandolin. The top line represents the "E" strings; the bottom line represents the "G" strings.*

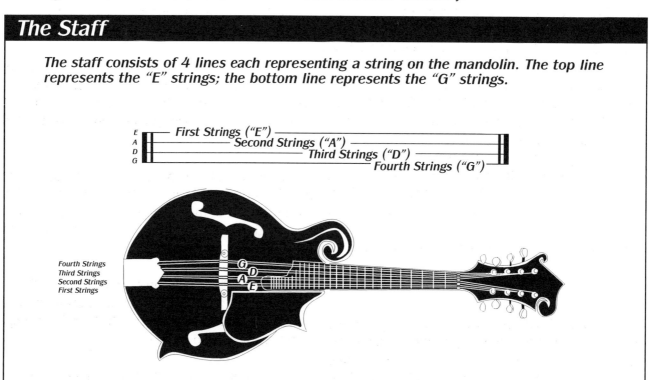

## The Numbers

*Every note is indicated by a number representing the distance of the fret from the nut. For instance: A "O" indicates that the string is to be played open, while a "3" indicates that the finger is to be placed behind the 3rd fret before picking the string.*

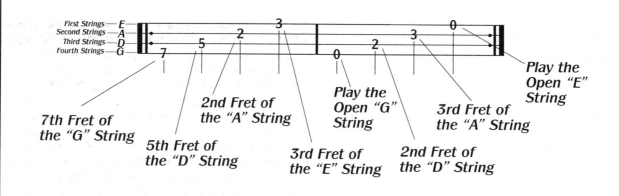

# Mandolin Fretboard & Tablature Timing

## Mandolin Fretboard

*The mandolin fretboard corresponds very easily to tablature staff. An example of the first 5 frets are illustrated below with the corresponding number indications for tablature.*

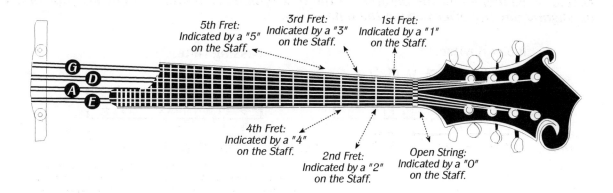

## Tablature Timing

*All forms of music notation has a system of symbols that translates the rhythm and timing of a song. Tablature borrows these symbols from standard notation so that it becomes a complete music language and can stand on its own without the player having to hear a recording of the piece before attempting to play it. Most all of the tunes in this book follow the standard 4 beats per measure with each beat represented by a quarter note. This is indicated at the beginning of each piece by a $\frac{4}{4}$ symbol. The top number represents how many beats per measure and the bottom number the type of note that receives the beat. For our uses, you will only be required to tap your foot four times for each measure.*

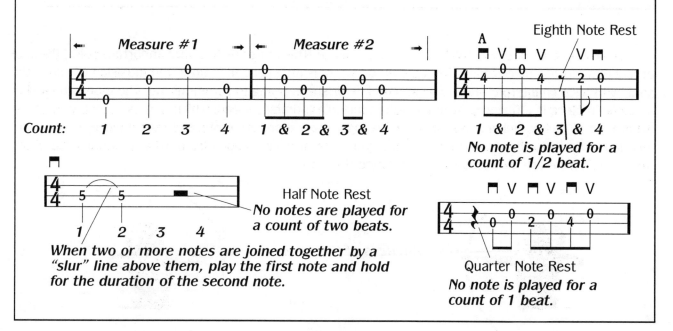

# Mandolin Tablature Timing

## Timing (cont.)

*One way to ensure that you're playing in correct timing is by keeping your eye on the Down & Up Stroke symbols. If a note is joined to another with a slur note, you'll only see one stroke symbol for the first note; the duration of the following note is only held for the sustain of the first note. Anytime you see a rest symbol following a note directly, the note should be deadened for the duration of the rest symbol. To do this, simply lift your finger up slightly directly after picking the note.*

Triplet Rhythm:                                 Missing Note:

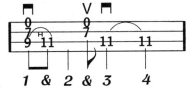

Count:    1 & a 2 & a 3 &          Count:    1 & 2 & 3    4

The second beat has no note which gives an 8th note pause before picking the & (off beat). The off beat here is picked with an up stroke which will fall rhythmically into the following down stroke on the 3rd beat.

Rest Symbols:

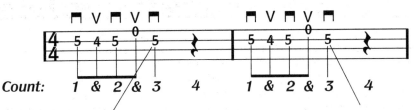

Count:    1 & 2 & 3    4    1 & 2 & 3    4

These notes are only held for one beat and followed with lifting the finger so that the note does not ring out for the fourth beat.

Timing is very relative to the feel of a musical piece. This brings us to a very important point, the soul or feel of a musical piece cannot be captured by symbols on a page. It is up to the musician to infuse the song with his own interpretation of what mood he or she is trying to communicate. The mood and feel of a mandolin piece is influenced by many factors including: timing, speed, which note is accented, medium (what type of pick is being used), gauge of strings, etc. Before attempting to read a piece, it is recommended to listen to the musical piece so that you at least have a good idea of what it sounds like. From there, you'll have artistic license for interpreting the piece.

    *Timing is of the Essence*

# Mandolin Tablature Pick Strokes

## Pick Strokes

There are only two pick strokes that can be accomplished with a flatpick: the "up stroke" and the "down stroke". In most flatpicking instances the down stroke would be played on the down beat and the up stroke would be played on the off beat. This is fairly consistent with crosspicking, although there are also many instances where the down beat would be played by an up stroke depending on the pattern involved. Below is an example of the standard approach including pick stroke symbols.

⊓ = Down Stroke

V = Up Stroke

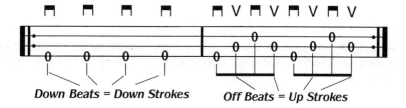

Down Beats = Down Strokes

Off Beats = Up Strokes

**NOTE:** Because crosspicking is very dependent on what direction is the pick stroke, all pieces and exercises include the pick stroke symbols for up and down. The rhythm and feel of the piece is established by the pick direction. Notes that fall naturally under an accent are accommodated by the pick stroke which greatly influences which notes are emphasized.

## The Metronome

The metronome is a very useful tool for determining the tempo of a tune. Of course the alternative is to listen to the piece being performed and match the tempo from the recording. The metronome is still a great tool for other purposes such as learning to keep good time. Each arrangement in this book has a box with the target tempo indicated by a quarter note followed by an "=" and a number. The number is the setting for the metronome. Target tempo is what you will be striving for as you practice. Normally you'll have to start out playing the arrangement slowly and gain speed as you become comfortable with the arrangement.

*The ultimate speed of the piece is indicated by the metronome setting. Start slowly and work up to the metronome setting.*

| Target Tempo: |
| ♩ = 200 |

This metronome setting is for 200. Each quarter note (♩) represents one beat. The number will always equal how many beats occur within one minute.

# Mandolin Tablature Chording

## Tablature Symbols

It is not necessary to attempt to memorize all of the symbols at this point. Just glance over them now and when encountering them in the arrangements refer back to this section for clarification.

### Chord Indications

*Chord indications are placed above the arrangement and establish the progression of the piece. It helps to become familiar with the chord progression before attempting to learn the arrangement.*

*Chord Symbols are Placed Directly Above the Measure*

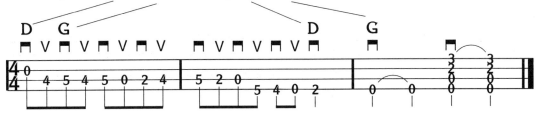

The below excerpt shows an Em ending chord that is strummed with a down stroke. It is strummed only once and held for two beats.

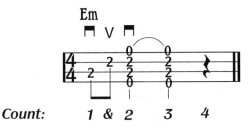

# Mandolin Tablature Endings

## Endings

Many tunes have "First Endings" and "Second Endings" that are indicated by the numbers "1" and "2". To properly play through these endings, simply return to the double dot upon playing the "First Ending"; while playing through it a second time, skip the "First Ending" playing only the "Second Ending" and, unless otherwise indicated, continue on through the piece.

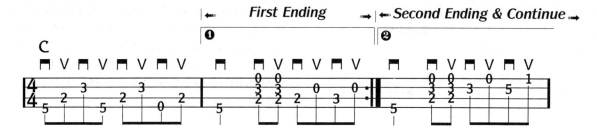

Song Endings are indicated by double lines without dots. At this point, you may optionally start the piece over or call it a take.

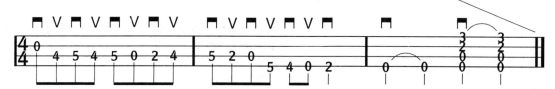

Section Endings are indicated by two dots—at this point, go back to the beginning of the section where the two dots start and repeat the entire section one time. Continue past the two dots after repeating the section.

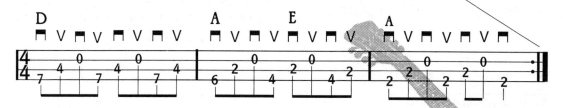

# Mandolin Tablature Symbols

## Attack Symbols

*The following indications are for the many ways that a string can be attacked (played) by the flatpick. These embellishments add color, texture and variety to the musical piece.*

### HAMMER-ONS

Hammer-ons are indicated by an "H" and a slur line. A hammer-on will always be going up in pitch not down.

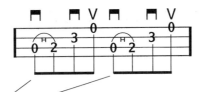

*The first note is picked with a down stroke while the second note is created with a forceful hammer with the fretting finger.*

### PULL-OFFS

Pull-offs are indicated by a "P" and a slur line. Pull-offs are essentially the reverse of hammer-ons. Your fretting hand will pull off of the designated note and string, thereby creating the following note/s without picking the string but once.

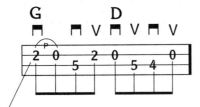

*The first note is picked with a down stroke while the second note is created with a pull-off motion of the fretting finger.*

### HARMONICS

Harmonics are created by lightly touching the string with your left finger while at the same time picking the string with your right hand. Natural harmonics can only be created at designated fret positions that divide the distance from the nut to the bridge.

*Harmonics are indicated by a down stroke symbol with a dot in the center.*

### SLIDES

Slides are indicated by an "S" with a diagonal line between two notes. Simply slide your fretting finger up to the next note indicated after picking the first note.

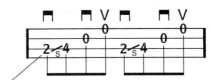

*Slides are indicated by a slash with an "S" underneath. In this example, pick the first note as a down stroke and then slide up to the 4th fret on the off beat.*

# Chord Diagrams

## Chords

*Chord inversions (positions) are laid out in both tablature and chord diagrams. Whenever you see more than one number aligned in tablature, you will be playing a chord (notes simultaneously played). Be careful to pay attention to the down or up stroke indicated when playing chords.*

### TABLATURE CHORD INDICATIONS

When you see any numbers placed on top of one another, a chord position is being illustrated.

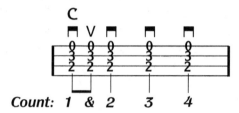

Count: 1 & 2 3 4

*All down stroke symbols designate that the chord is to be strummed in a downward motion, the up stoke symbol requires that the chord be strummed in an upward motion.*

### CHORD DIAGRAMS

Chord diagrams are on every preparatory study page. By careful study and use of the hand positions illustrated, the arrangements are less difficult to deal with.

❶ =First Finger

❷ =Second Finger

❸ =Third Finger

❹ =Fourth Finger

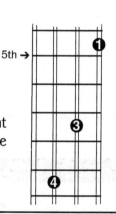

5th →

A number with an arrow indicates what fret position that the chord starts at.

*Each exercise page displays chord positions that are utilized throughout the studies and songs. Open strings utilized (not fretted by the left hand) will be indicated on the tablature by "O's".*

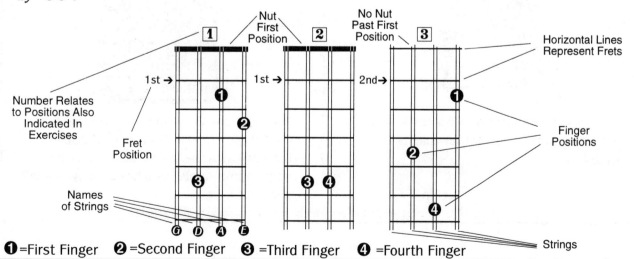

❶=First Finger ❷=Second Finger ❸=Third Finger ❹=Fourth Finger

# Useful Tools

## More On The Metronome

Invented by J. N. Mälzel in 1816, the metronome is invaluable during the learning process. Not only does it measure the exact tempo of the arrangements enclosed (settings are indicated at the top of each piece), but it becomes an indispensable tool for measuring your progress with the exercises and studies. By starting out on low settings, you'll be able to learn the exercise with an even tempo establishing a good foundation for playing the exercises up-tempo.

The metronome will also give you an inner sense of good timing that will reflect whenever you get together with other musicians. Keep a metronome by your side whenever you're practicing!

## Picks

Picks come in many sizes, thicknesses and shapes. Crosspicking demands a lot of a pick. Try to avoid picks that are too thin (light) for they have no projection and slap with a clicking sound on the strings. Use a medium to heavy pick for better volume and more control. As far as size is concerned, it should come down to personal preference. Even though, avoid using tiny picks; they don't have much area to grab a string which can cause a loss in dynamic control. Smaller picks are less likely to attack both unison strings on a mandolin. You need to be able to get behind the strings with a medium to large-size pick in order to pluck both unison strings. The character of the mandolin is lost when only one of the unison strings are being struck by the pick.

---

### Types of Metronomes

| Traditional Pendulum Version | Modern-Day Electronic Version |
|---|---|
| 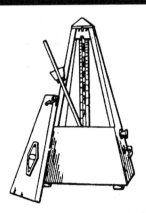 | 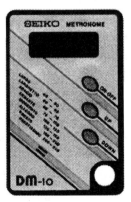 |
| This version operates by a windup pendulum along with a weight that adjusts the speed. | This digital version operates by touchpad controls and consists of an LCD Display that indicates the tempo along with an audio output emitting a beep for every beat. |

*This is only a sampling of the many varieties of metronomes available today.*

# Right Hand Technique

## Right-Hand Position

There are as many ways as the right hand is positioned as there are mandolin players. Many of the positions limit the right hand from moving freely. This restricts the playing capability of the right hand and will limit speed and dexterity. With crosspicking, it is critical that the right hand is loosely positioned above the strings so that it can move completely free of any obstruction. For instance, many mandolin players rest the heel of the hand on the bridge; this restricts the right-hand picking movement and does not allow the hand to take advantage of playing closer to the fingerboard for a mellower tone.

Crosspicking technique can be accomplished efficiently by keeping the wrist loose. Imagine trying to jump from string to string for every other note with a stiff wrist. Although, it can be done, your whole forearm has to move for every note; whereas, with a loose wrist, the movement is much more concentrated and can be easily accomplished with minimal movement. The forearm does not need to be completely stationary, in fact, by playing with both a loose wrist and forearm you'll have optimal movement for speed and efficiency.

## How to Properly Hold Your Pick

There are many ways that the pick is welded. Some contribute to effective technique while many others will impede technique. After getting comfortable with playing with a loose wrist, how you hold your pick should fall into place. No two players have the exact same muscle and build for hands and arms. Therefore, what works for one individual may not work for another. There still are common principles that apply to everyone.

1. You should never have to grab your pick tightly. This will only tighten up your muscles unnecessarily and will reflect in your playing with tension and tightness.

2. You should never choke your pick to the point that there's a limited surface for it to strike the string. This will minimize the ability to utilize dynamics (volume control), will limit accuracy, and will make it difficult to strike both strings of one chorus simultaneously.

3. The pick angle should always be flat in relation to the strings. If not, you'll gain transients (pick noise) as the pick rubs against wound strings. Sometimes, you'll want this effect to utilize as coloring, but usually on rare occasion.

---

### Wrist Loosening Exercise

*When throwing a Frisbee, or dealing out a deck of cards, the wrist is usually completely loose in the process. Now apply this same looseness to your mandolin by playing a tremolo on each string. A tremolo is a rapid down-and-up movement of the pick against a string that will give the impression of a long continuous tone. Your forearm will move slightly in the process even with your wrist completely loose. Practice this technique until you feel confident that you're playing with a loose wrist. If you're tiring quickly, you're probably not using enough wrist movement and need to focus on being totally relaxed when approaching this exercise. You'll know you've accomplished the exercise properly when you do not tire easily and find yourself playing the tremolo without any concentrated effort.*

# Crosspicking Exercises

## Introductory Two-String Crosspicking

The following exercises will establish a solid foundation for the crosspicking arrangements to follow. It is critical to develop good right-hand technique in order to crosspick with total independence. Accomplish these exercises in the order that they are given before attempting any of the arrangements in this book.

The first exercise involves only the right hand; no left-hand fretting will be required. This exercise will allow you to focus on right-hand movement without the distraction of having to fret with the left hand. This exercise pattern is designed to give the impression of a tremolo (or continuous tone), hence the name: Tremolo Two-String Crosspicking.

### Tremolo Two-String Crosspicking I:

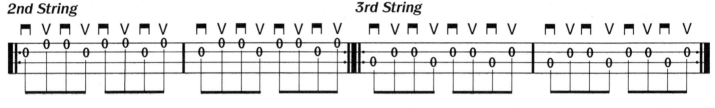

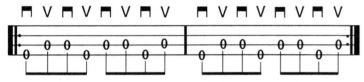

### Two-String Tremolo

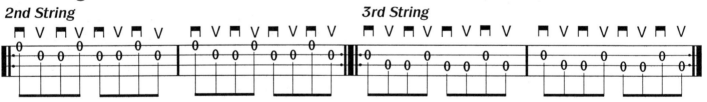

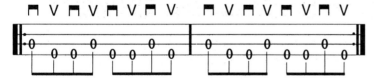

Before moving on to other studies, try playing these exercises with your eyes closed. You should be able to cross over from exercise to exercise without stopping or accidentally hitting the wrong string. Once you're comfortable with this pattern and have it completely memorized, you may continue onward.

## Exercises In 6ths

The following exercises introduces the G Scale ascending and descending in sixths. If you've memorized the preceding exercises, you now should only have to concentrate on fretting the positions with the left hand.

### Two-String Tremolo Variation as Applied to a G scale in 6ths

**Ascending**

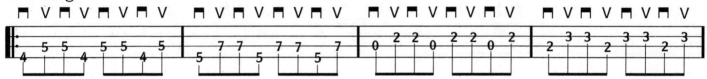

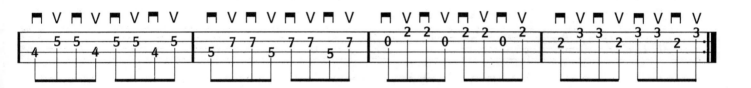

**Descending**

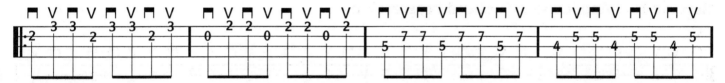

Upon completing the preceding exercises, apply the Inverted Tremolo Two-String Crosspicking Pattern #II to the same ascending and descending G Scale. Another exercise that will guarantee that you're completely comfortable with these tremolo patterns would be to move all of the ascending and descending G 6th Scale up two frets. This would put you in the Key of A. This pattern will remain relatively consistent no matter what key you try it in.

# Crosspicking Exercises

## Reverse Rolls

We are now going to focus on the many other crosspicking patterns that will be utilized throughout the book. After learning these patterns thoroughly, we'll be applying them to chord progressions so that you'll be developing your left and right hand coordination.

**Reverse Roll 3rd String**          **Reverse Roll 4th String**

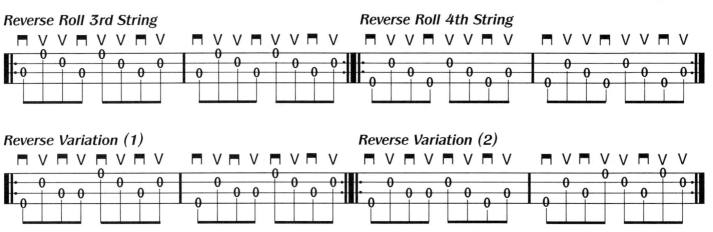

*Reverse Variation (1)*          *Reverse Variation (2)*

## Reverse Roll Applied to a G Chord Progression

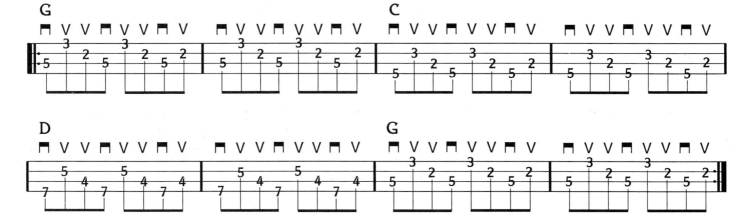

## Reverse Rolls

All of these variations may be applied to any number of chord progressions you'd like to try. A surefire way to become comfortable with these rolls is to experiment with them within other chord progressions before moving on. Always consider the many possibilities that await you after memorizing these rolls. Try adding new life to old songs by applying them within familiar contexts.

### Reverse Variation (1)

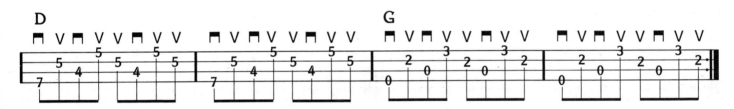

### Reverse Variation (2)

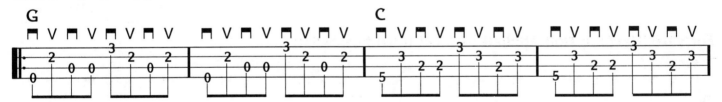

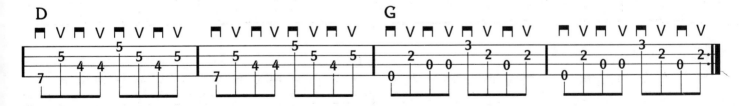

# Crosspicking Exercises

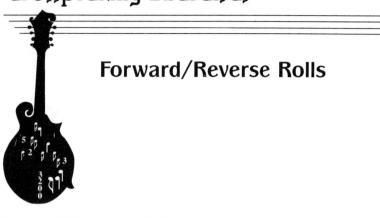

## Forward/Reverse Rolls

### Forward/Reverse Roll
*3rd String*                                        *4th String*

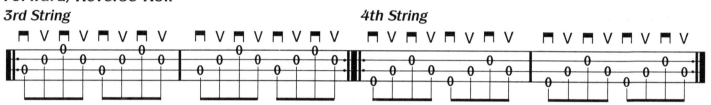

### Reverse/Forward
*3rd String*                                        *4th String*

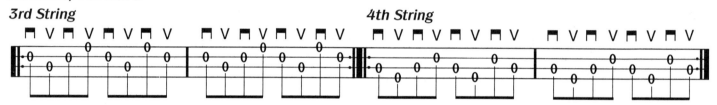

### Forward/Reverse Roll Applied to a G Chord Progression

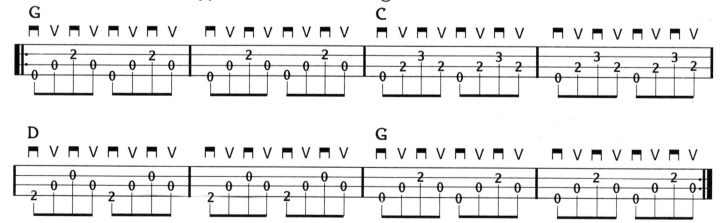

## Forward/Reverse Rolls

### Forward/Reverse Applied to a D Chord Progression

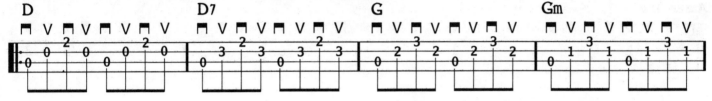

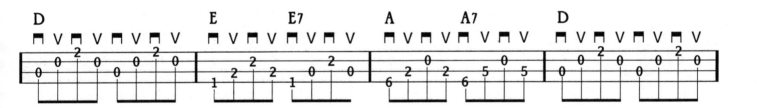

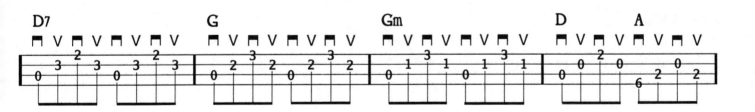

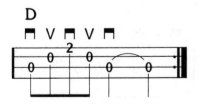

# Crosspicking Exercises

## Exercises In 3rds

**Two-String Tremolo Variation (2) as applied to G scale in 3rds**

*Ascending*

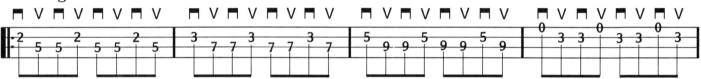

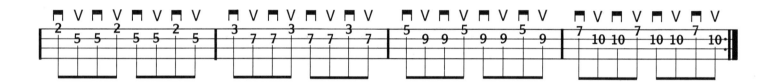

*Descending*

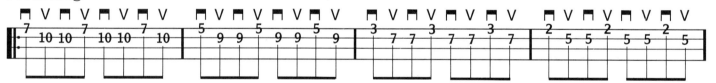

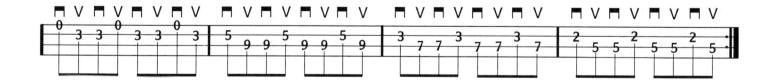

## Exercises In Octaves

**Tremolo Variation (1) as applied to G scale in Octaves**

*Ascending*

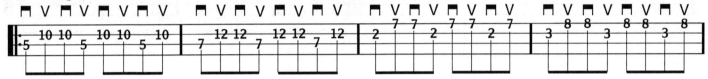

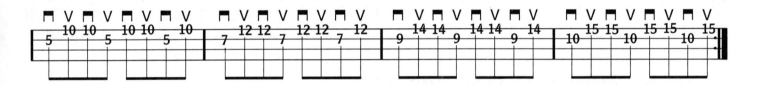

*Descending*

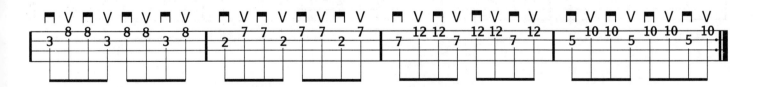

# Crosspicking Exercises

## Forward Rolls

### Forward Roll 3rd String

### Forward Roll 4th String

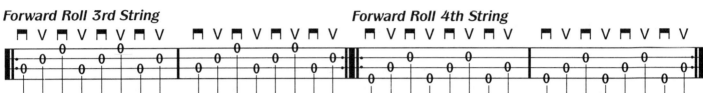

### Variations on Forward Roll

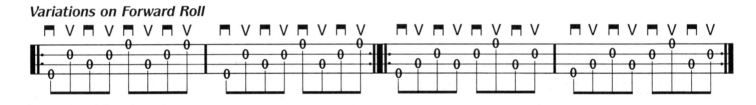

## Forward Roll applied to a G chord Progression

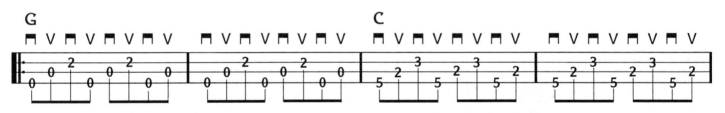

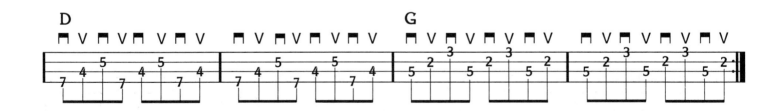

## Forward Rolls

### Forward Roll Variation (1)

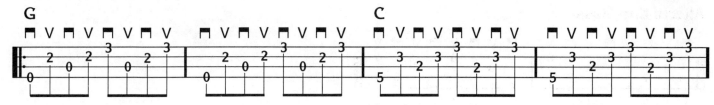

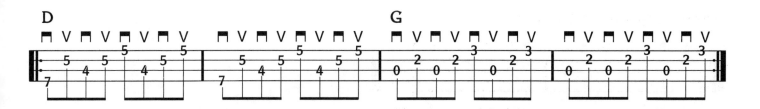

### Forward Roll Variation (2)

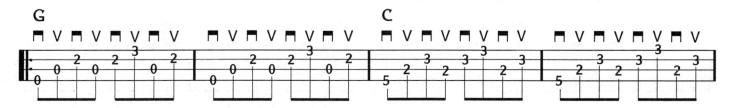

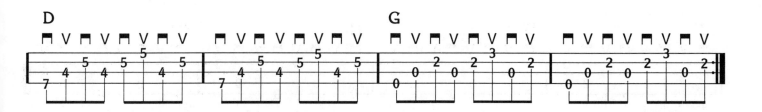

# Crosspicking Exercises

## Alternating Bass

### Alternating Bass

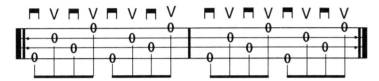

### Alternating Bass Variation

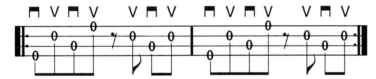

### Alternating Bass Over a C Chord Progression

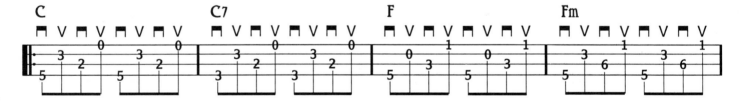

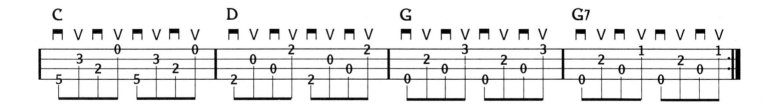

## Alternating Bass

### Alternating Bass Variaton Over a C Chord Progression

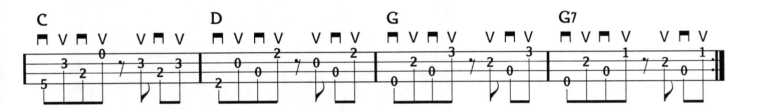

### Alternating Bass Variaton Over a G Chord Progression

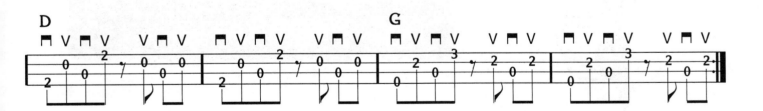

**1941 Gibson F-5**

***Become one with your instrument.***

# *Crosspicking Bluegrass Style*

## Wildwood Flower

## Home Sweet Home

## Under the Double Eagle

## John Hardy

## Redwing

## Grandfather's Clock

# Wildwood Flower
# Preparatory Study Notes

**General Guidelines:** Because of the many forward and reverse rolls utilized throughout, this arrangement has bluegrass banjo overtones. Keep the rhythm even and be careful not to rush the notes. The forward rolls can have a tendency to jump ahead of the tempo since they are easier to perform fast. If you're not practicing along with a metronome, try tapping your foot to ensure an even rhythm. Above all, accomplish all of the preparatory study notes before attempting the piece itself.

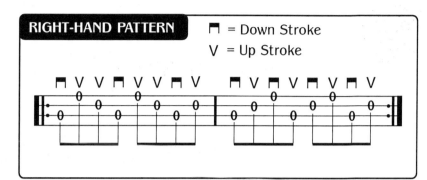

**RIGHT-HAND PATTERN** ⊓ = Down Stroke  V = Up Stroke

**RIGHT-HAND PATTERN WITH CHORD EXERCISE**

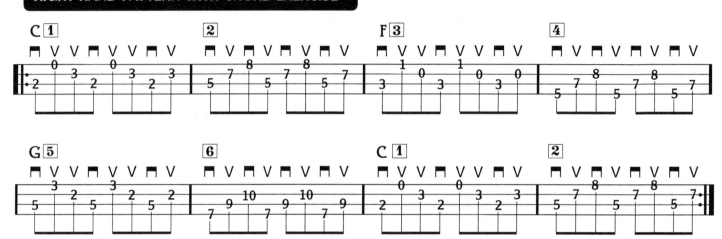

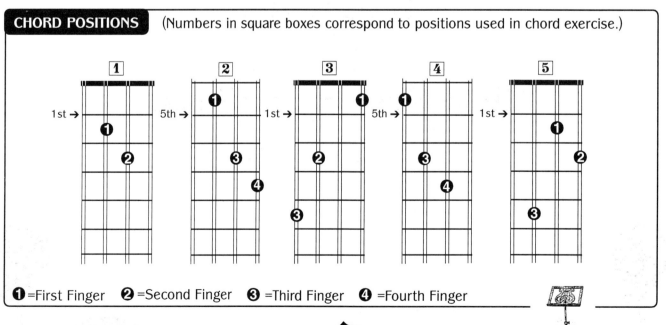

**CHORD POSITIONS** (Numbers in square boxes correspond to positions used in chord exercise.)

1st → / 5th → / 1st → / 5th → / 1st →

❶=First Finger   ❷=Second Finger   ❸=Third Finger   ❹=Fourth Finger

# Wildwood Flower
# Preparatory Study Notes (cont.)

## RIGHT-HAND PATTERN

◰ = Down Stroke

V = Up Stroke

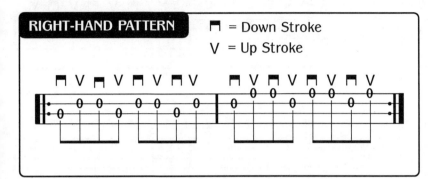

*Of Noted Interest:* The Carter Family had written many songs which today are considered standards. "Wildwood Flower" was quickly adapted as "the first tune to learn on acoustic guitar" by generations of folk guitarists. Mother Maybelle Carter does a beautiful autoharp rendition of this melody on the historic *Will The circle Be Unbroken* recording produced by William McEuen.

## RIGHT-HAND PATTERN WITH CHORD EXERCISE

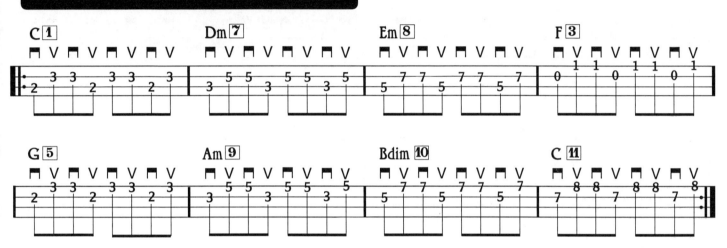

## CHORD POSITIONS

(Numbers in square boxes correspond to positions used in chord exercise.)

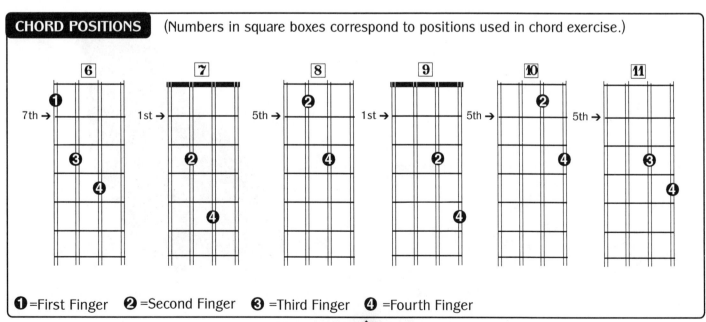

❶ =First Finger    ❷ =Second Finger    ❸ =Third Finger    ❹ =Fourth Finger

# Wildwood Flower

(A.P. CARTER)

Target Tempo:
♩ = 165

Key of C

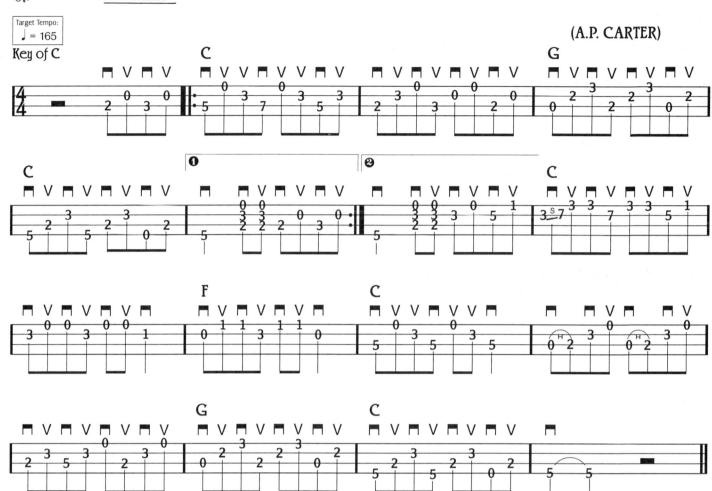

## A Diverse Selection of Mandolins

# Home Sweet Home
# Preparatory Study Notes

**General Guidelines:** Before attempting the chord exercise, the right-hand pattern should be memorized and mastered. Keep the tempo even—there should be no pause whatsoever between any of the notes. Start off slowly, don't rush. Make sure you have all of the chord patterns memorized and can switch between them comfortably and efficiently. Notice how a few of the finger positions can remain stationary when switching from chord to chord. All that is required is to slide the fingers to the new position.

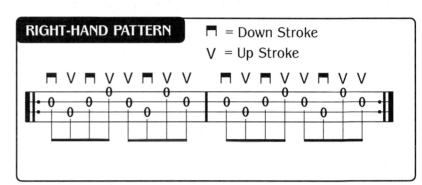

## RIGHT-HAND PATTERN WITH CHORD EXERCISE

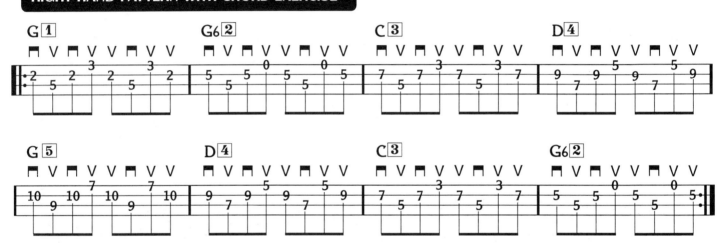

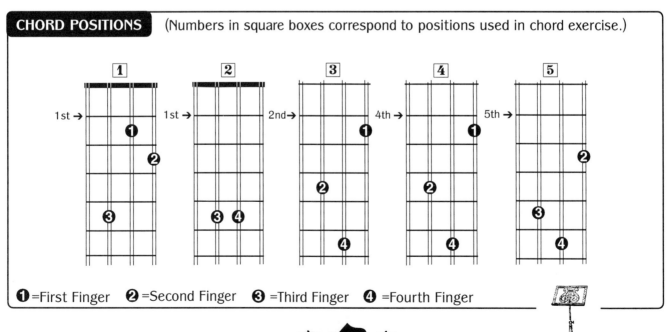

**❶**=First Finger   **❷**=Second Finger   **❸**=Third Finger   **❹**=Fourth Finger

# Home Sweet Home
## Preparatory Study Notes (cont.)

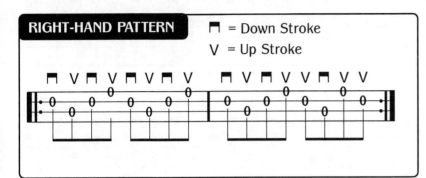

**RIGHT-HAND PATTERN**

⊓ = Down Stroke
V = Up Stroke

*Of Noted Interest:* Dan Crary performs crosspicking guitar in a powerful way. His arrangement of "Home Sweet Home" in *Deacon Dan Crary's Flatpicking Guitar Technique* book is simple and effective. Glean new ideas by listening and studying at every opportunity to how a guitarist arranges and performs crosspicking.

**RIGHT-HAND PATTERN WITH CHORD EXERCISE**

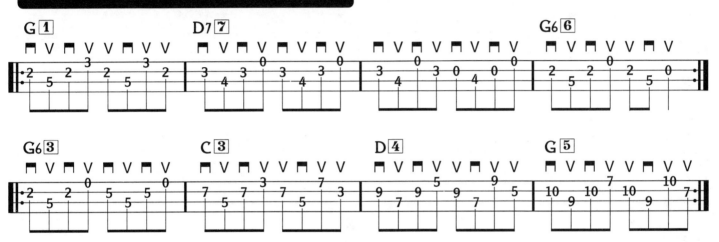

**CHORD POSITIONS** (Numbers in square boxes correspond to positions used in chord exercise.)

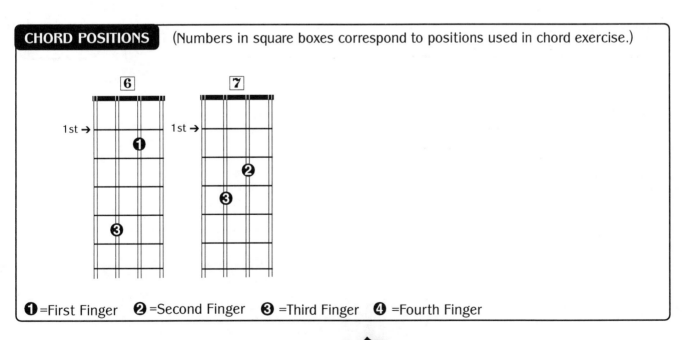

❶ =First Finger   ❷ =Second Finger   ❸ =Third Finger   ❹ =Fourth Finger

# Home Sweet Home

Target Tempo:
♩ = 155

Key of G

*'Mid pleasures and palaces though we may roam,*
*Be it ever so humble, there's no place like home.*

**—Home, Sweet Home. From the opera**
**Clari, The Maid of Milan (1823).**

# Under The Double Eagle
# Preparatory Study Notes

**General Guidelines:** Play this tune at a moderate pace with a "march" feel. Notice the "ragtime turn-around" in part II with the B6 chord! Try experimenting with other rolls over this same chord pattern.

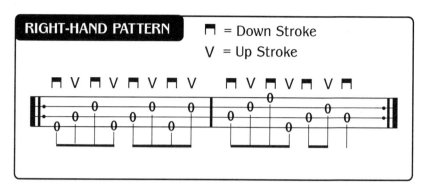

## RIGHT-HAND PATTERN WITH CHORD EXERCISE

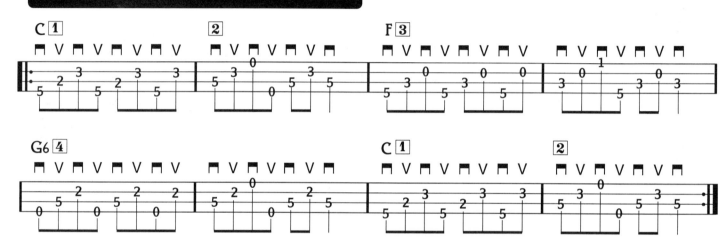

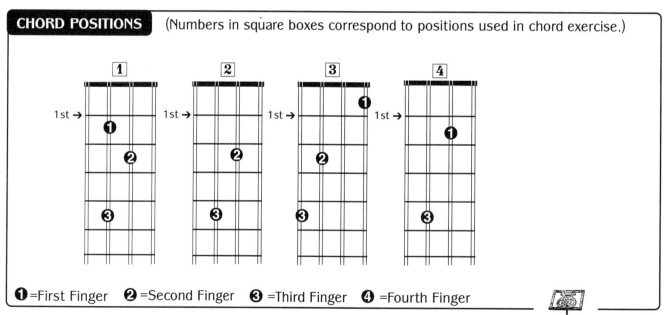

❶ =First Finger    ❷ =Second Finger    ❸ =Third Finger    ❹ =Fourth Finger

# Under The Double Eagle
# Preparatory Study Notes (cont.)

*Of Noted Interest:* Composed by Josef Franz Wagner in 1903 for marching band, this tune has been adapted by other genres and probably has had thousands of conceived arrangements. The original composition consisted of four parts. Today, the standard arrangement only consists of two parts.

**RIGHT-HAND PATTERN**

⊓ = Down Stroke
V = Up Stroke

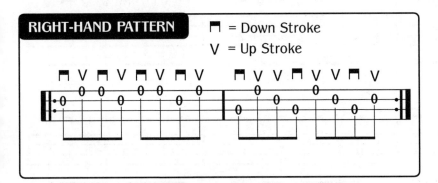

**RIGHT-HAND PATTERN WITH CHORD EXERCISE**

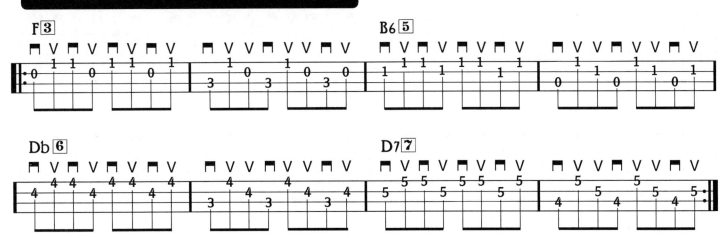

**CHORD POSITIONS** (Numbers in square boxes correspond to positions used in chord exercise.)

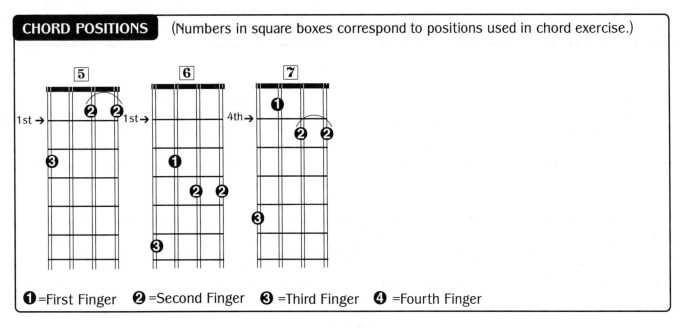

❶ =First Finger   ❷ =Second Finger   ❸ =Third Finger   ❹ =Fourth Finger

# Under The Double Eagle

(Josef Franz Wagner)

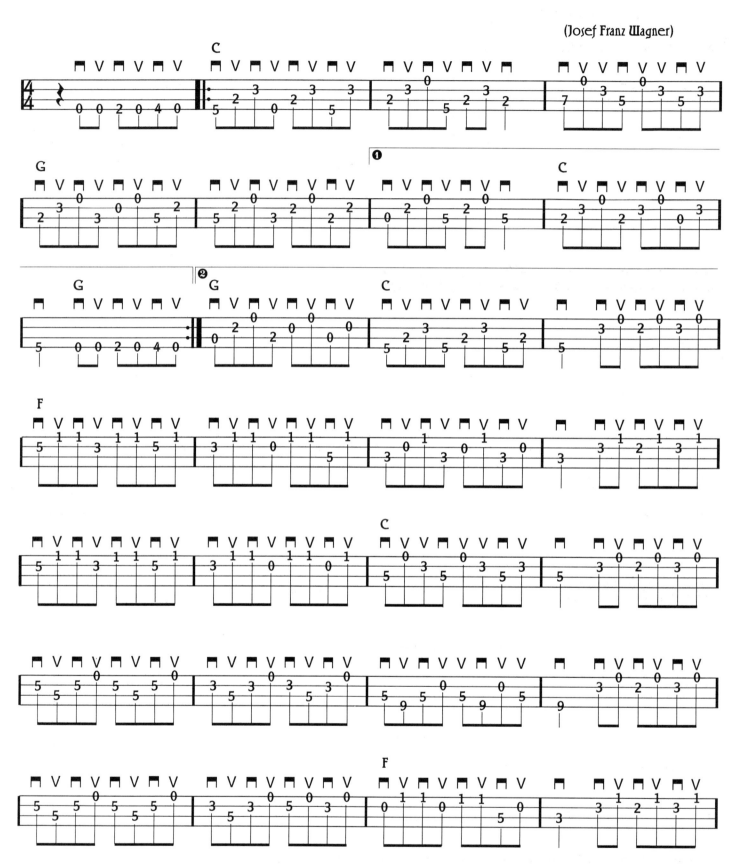

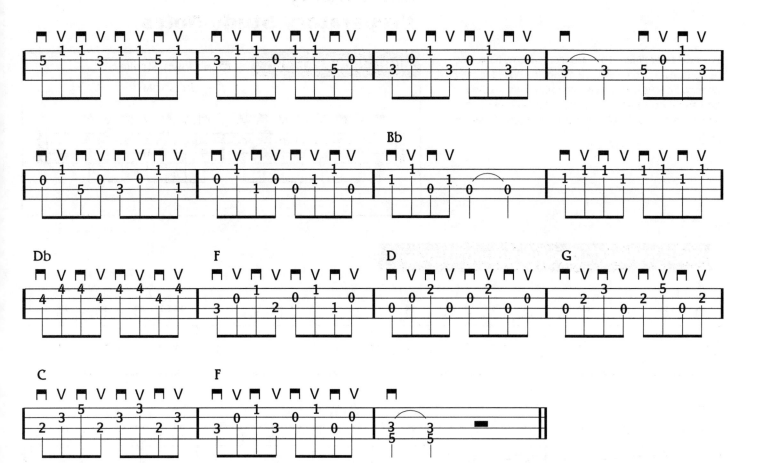

# John Hardy
# Preparatory Study Notes

*General Guidelines:* This arrangement is as banjoistic as you'll ever achieve with a mandolin. Based mostly on forward rolls, the tune is naturally up tempo. Again, be careful no to let your tempo fluctuate especially since the forward roll can sometimes get ahead of you.

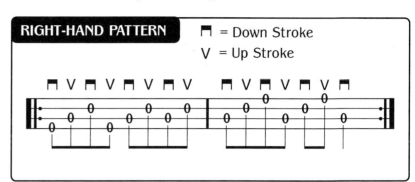

## RIGHT-HAND PATTERN WITH CHORD EXERCISE

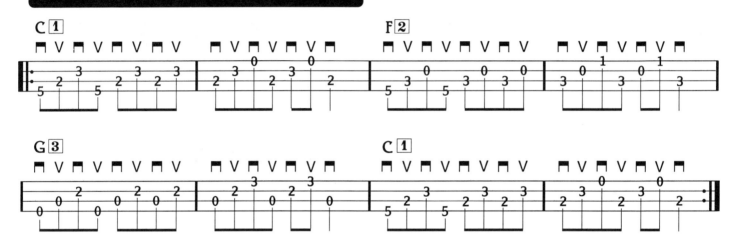

**CHORD POSITIONS** (Numbers in square boxes correspond to positions used in chord exercise.)

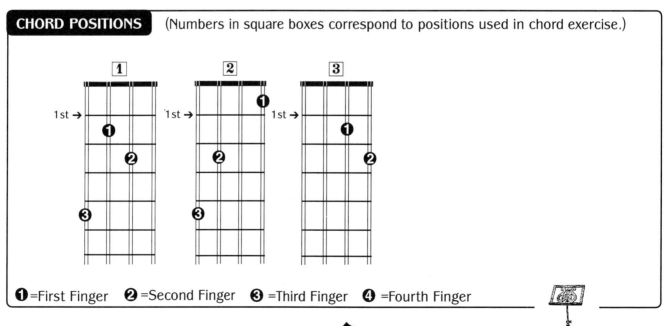

❶=First Finger  ❷=Second Finger  ❸=Third Finger  ❹=Fourth Finger

# John Hardy
# Preparatory Study Notes (cont.)

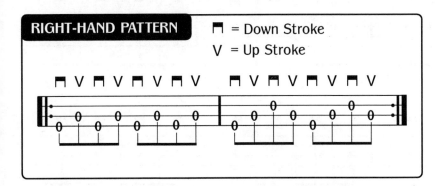

**RIGHT-HAND PATTERN**

⊓ = Down Stroke
V = Up Stroke

*Of Noted Interest:* This American ballad, about a murderer who was Afro-American named John Hardy, is now a rousing bluegrass instrumental. It's said that John Hardy himself wrote the tune awaiting his stand with the gallows pole.

**RIGHT-HAND PATTERN WITH CHORD EXERCISE**

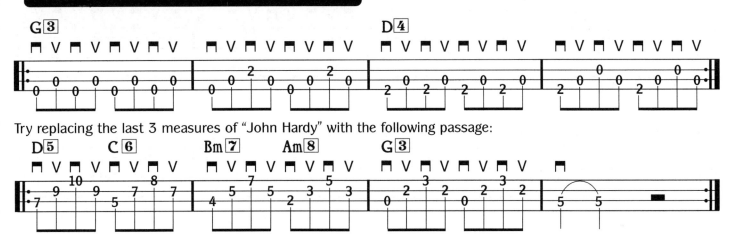

Try replacing the last 3 measures of "John Hardy" with the following passage:

**CHORD POSITIONS** (Numbers in square boxes correspond to positions used in chord exercise.)

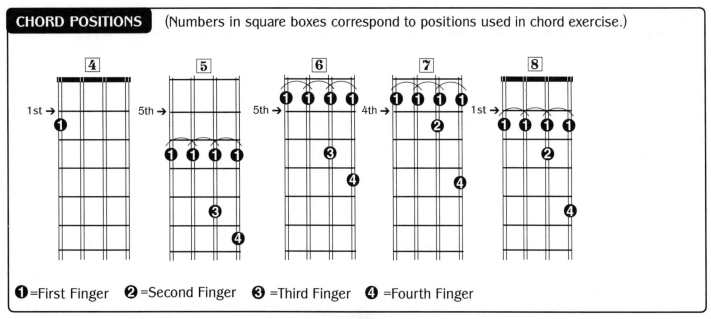

❶=First Finger  ❷=Second Finger  ❸=Third Finger  ❹=Fourth Finger

# John Hardy

To Beginning...

They took John Hardy to the hangin' ground,
They hung him there to die.
The very last words that poor boy said,
'My forty gun never told a lie, Lord, Lord . . .'

*—The Last Verse*
*from John Hardy*

# Red Wing
# Preparatory Study Notes

**General Guidelines:** The forward roll dominates this piece. Arranged to capture the feel of bluegrass banjo in "Scruggs' Style", the melody rides on the lower strings while the forward roll fills in the spaces with chordal harmonizations. Use your metronome for tempo insurance; the forward roll has a tendency to rush.

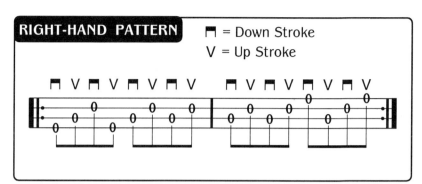

**RIGHT-HAND PATTERN WITH CHORD EXERCISE**

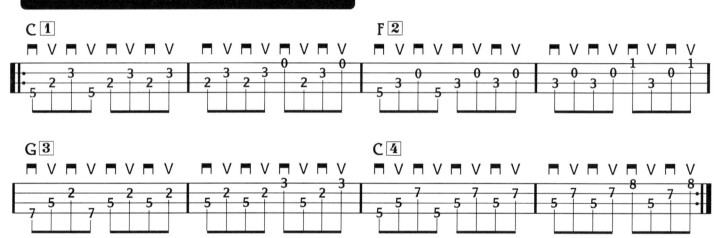

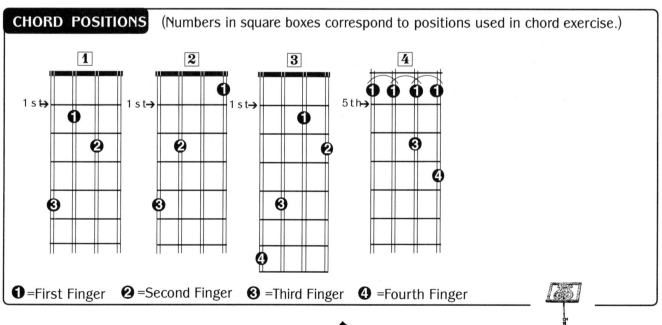

❶=First Finger   ❷=Second Finger   ❸=Third Finger   ❹=Fourth Finger

# Red Wing
# Preparatory Study Notes (cont.)

**RIGHT-HAND PATTERN**

◻ = Down Stroke
V = Up Stroke

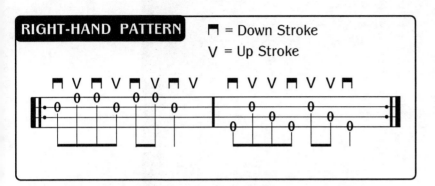

*Of Noted Interest:* I first learned this piece from Ray Valla's book *Deluxe Bluegrass Mandolin Method*. In fact, his influence permeates this particular arrangement—some of the fingering is very similar. If possible, learn his arrangement first and then attempt to learn this crosspicking arrangement. You'll gain a new perspective on arranging your own crosspicking pieces and even apply the techniques to pieces you already know.

**RIGHT-HAND PATTERN WITH CHORD EXERCISE**

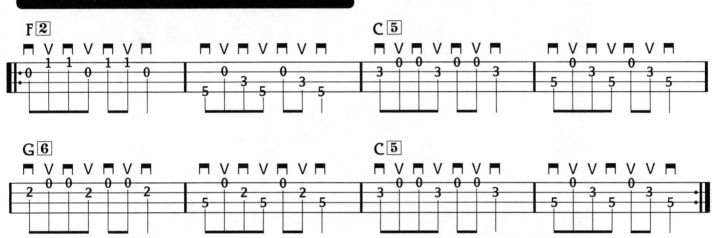

**CHORD POSITIONS** (Numbers in square boxes correspond to positions used in chord exercise.)

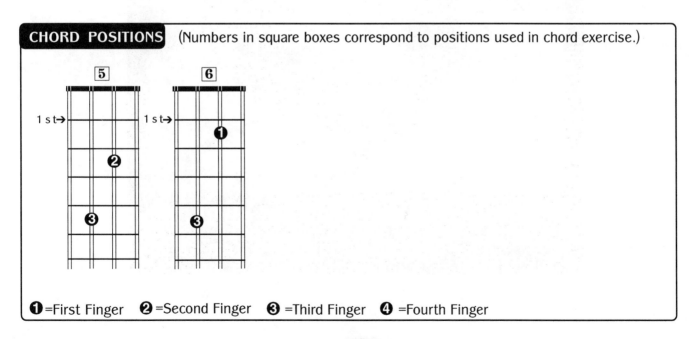

❶ =First Finger   ❷ =Second Finger   ❸ =Third Finger   ❹ =Fourth Finger

**Extremely Rare Epiphone Windsor Mandolin (1930s)**

# Red Wing

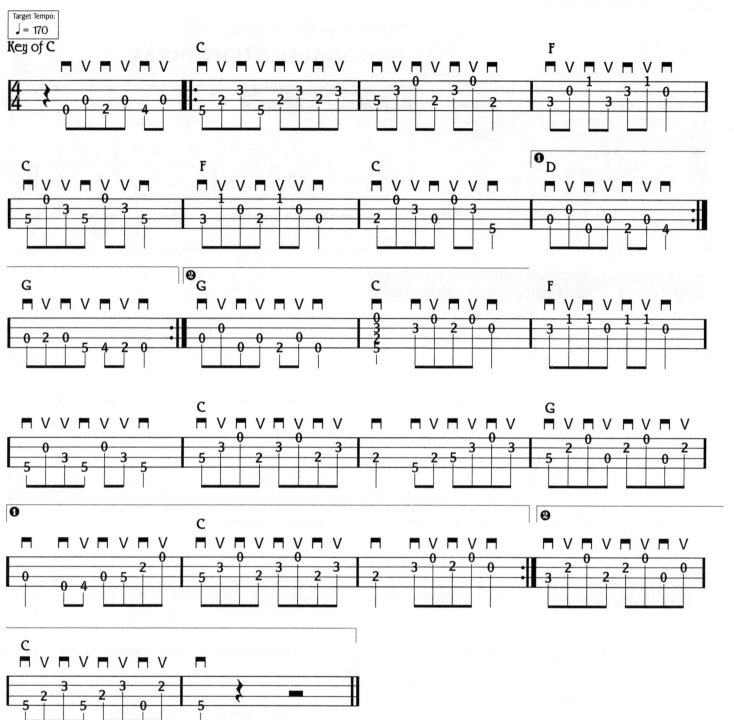

# Grandfather's Clock
# Preparatory Study Notes

**General Guidelines:** The second measure of this arrangement contains the most difficult chord position. Be careful to keep your fourth finger free and positioned over the 7th fret. (Use chord diagram #2) Play this tune with controlled patience. Remember, it's a song about a clock; you must not be impatient! Watch for the harmonics—they give the impression of the clock striking on the hour hand. You could also deaden the string (muting), thereby creating a "tick tock".

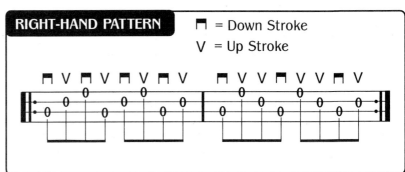

**RIGHT-HAND PATTERN**

⊓ = Down Stroke
V = Up Stroke

**RIGHT-HAND PATTERN WITH CHORD EXERCISE**

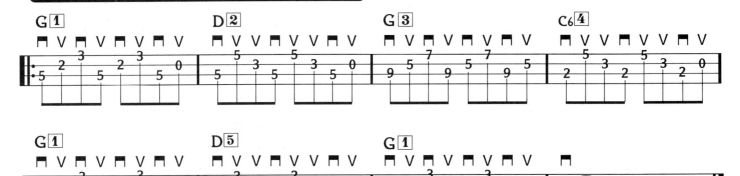

**CHORD POSITIONS** (Numbers in square boxes correspond to positions used in chord exercise.)

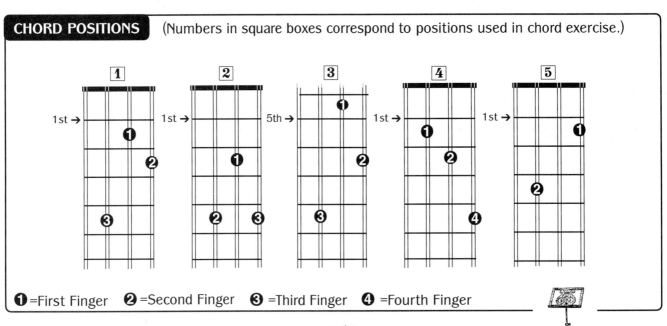

❶=First Finger  ❷=Second Finger  ❸=Third Finger  ❹=Fourth Finger

# Grandfather's Clock
# Preparatory Study Notes (cont.)

## RIGHT-HAND PATTERN

$\sqcap$ = Down Stroke

V = Up Stroke

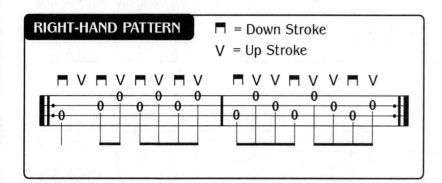

*Of Noted Interest:* This tune was written by Henry Work in 1876 and has undoubtedly outlived many a grandfather clock. "Grandfather's Clock" has had many arrangements created and performed on all kinds of instruments throughout its history. Yet, the one and only instrument that really breathes life into this time-less (no pun intended) piece is the banjo. Ergo, we've imitated the banjo roll on the mandolin—adapting "that" banjoistic sound to the mandolin for this time-honored piece.

## RIGHT-HAND PATTERN WITH CHORD EXERCISE

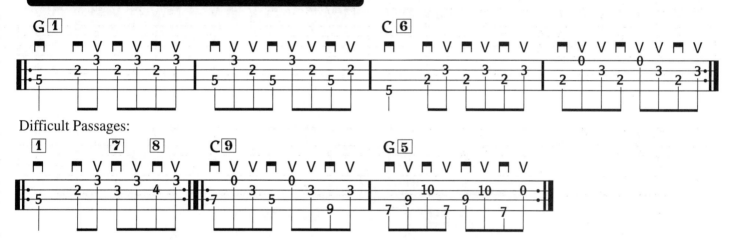

Difficult Passages:

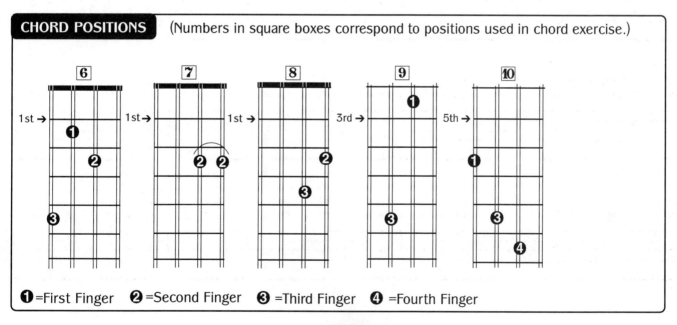

## CHORD POSITIONS    (Numbers in square boxes correspond to positions used in chord exercise.)

❶=First Finger     ❷=Second Finger     ❸=Third Finger     ❹=Fourth Finger

# Grandfather's Clock

(Henry Work)

Target Tempo:
♩ = 160

Key of G

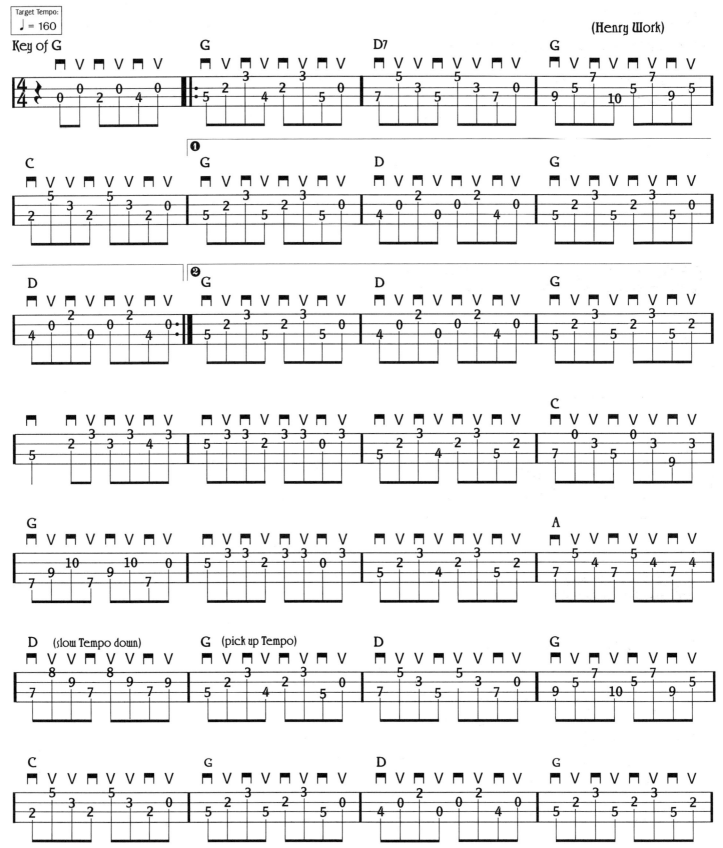

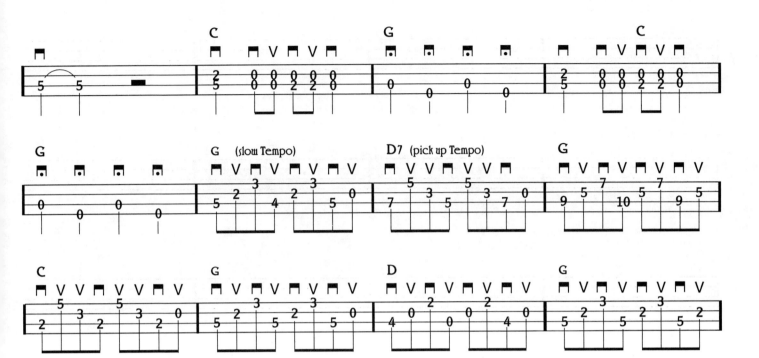

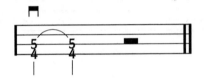

# *Crosspicking Fiddle Style*

**Boil Them Cabbage Down**

**Down Yonder**

**Fisher's Hornpipe**

**Eighth of January**

**Bald Headed End of the Broom**

**Soldier's Joy**

**Blackberry Blossom**

**Whiskey Before Breakfast**

# Boil Them Cabbage Down
# Preparatory Study Notes

*General Guidelines:* This arrangement emulates the classic fiddle shuffle rhythm. These patterns can easily be adapted to other fiddle tunes with similar shuffle rhythms like "Orange Blossom Special". If you've practiced your rolls thoroughly, especially as they apply to chord progressions, this arrangement will be relatively easy for you to accomplish.

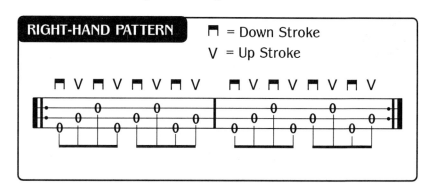

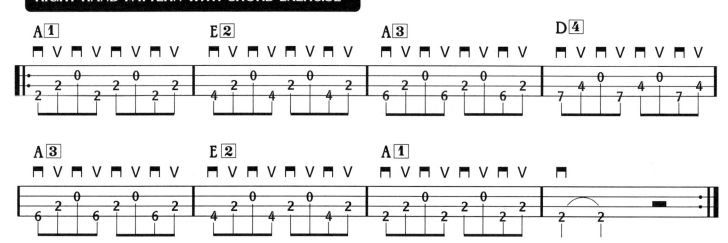

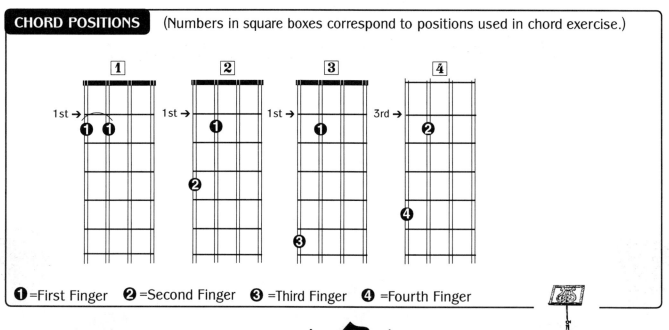

❶=First Finger  ❷=Second Finger  ❸=Third Finger  ❹=Fourth Finger

# Boil Them Cabbage Down
## Preparatory Study Notes (cont.)

**Of Noted Interest:** Legend has it that this tune was composed during the meeting of the two great railroads uniting the continental US by railway from the east coast to the west coast for the first time. During the celebration, they were boiling cabbage as a cure for the "morning after hangover"—hence the name of the tune. This tune also goes by the name of "Bile Them Cabbage Down".

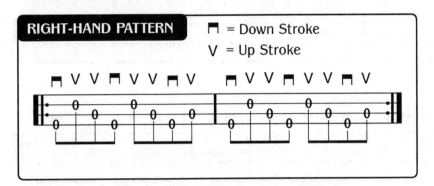

**RIGHT-HAND PATTERN**

◻ = Down Stroke
V = Up Stroke

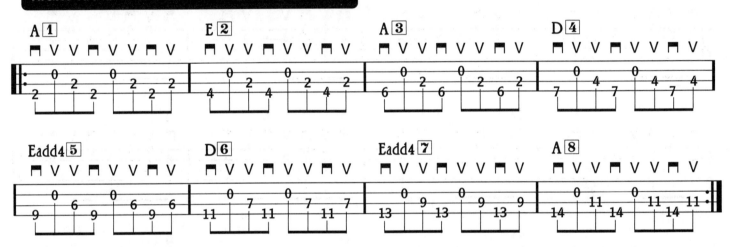

**RIGHT-HAND PATTERN WITH CHORD EXERCISE**

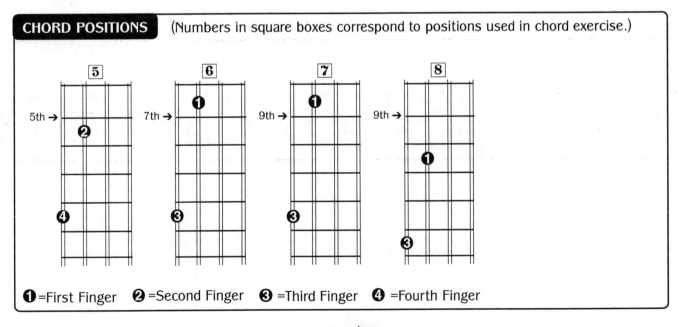

**CHORD POSITIONS** (Numbers in square boxes correspond to positions used in chord exercise.)

❶ =First Finger   ❷ =Second Finger   ❸ =Third Finger   ❹ =Fourth Finger

# Boil Them Cabbage Down

Target Tempo:
♩ = 200 Key of A

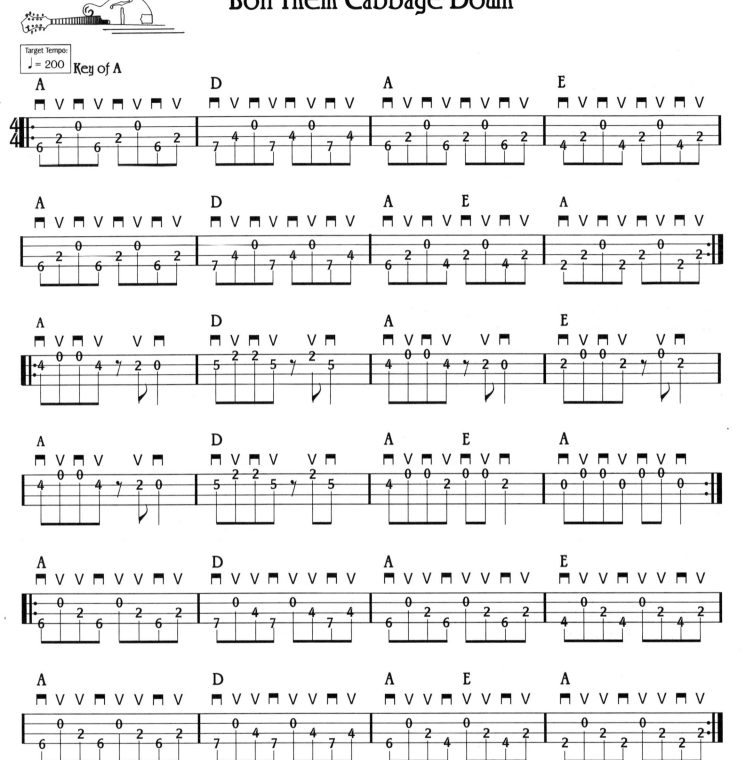

# Down Yonder
# Preparatory Study Notes

**General Guidelines:** The most difficult part of this arrangement for crosspicking mandolin involves each section's kickoff. These kickoffs involve two-finger chords—in fiddle lingo they would be called double-stops. Practice them over and over as illustrated in your preparatory notes, otherwise they may "bottle-neck" your tempo. Most of the crosspicking here involves a variation of the alternating bass roll.

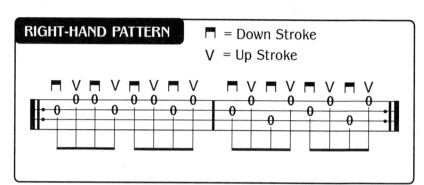

**RIGHT-HAND PATTERN WITH CHORD EXERCISE**

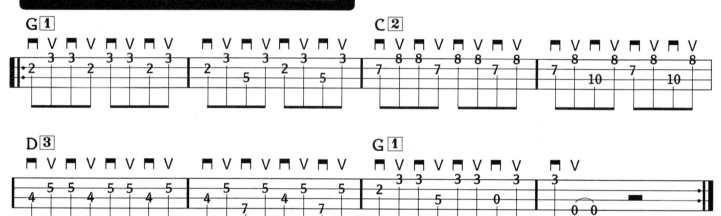

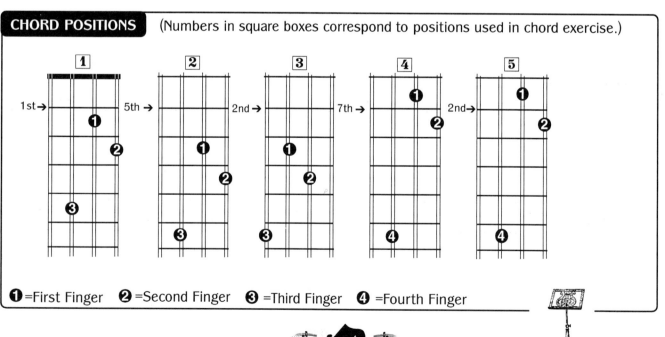

**❶**=First Finger  **❷**=Second Finger  **❸**=Third Finger  **❹**=Fourth Finger

# Down Yonder
# Preparatory Study Notes (cont.)

**General Guidelines:** Down Yonder was written by Gid Tanner and the Skillet Lickers from down Georgia way. Listen to the version on the *Will the Circle Be Unbroken* recording with the Nitty Gritty Dirt Band. It's an excellent rendition with Doc Watson leading it off with, "How does it go Vassar!"—giving the impression that it's the first take.

## RIGHT-HAND PATTERN

⊓ = Down Stroke

V = Up Stroke

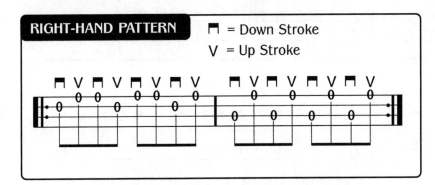

## RIGHT-HAND PATTERN WITH CHORD EXERCISE

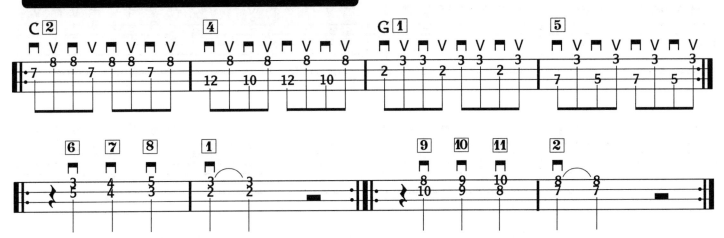

## CHORD POSITIONS

(Numbers in square boxes correspond to positions used in chord exercise.)

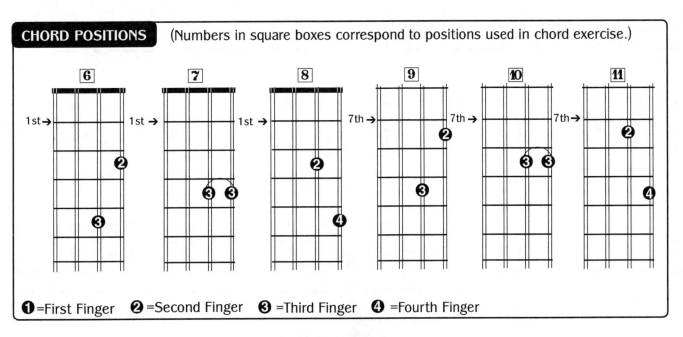

❶=First Finger   ❷=Second Finger   ❸=Third Finger   ❹=Fourth Finger

# Down Yonder

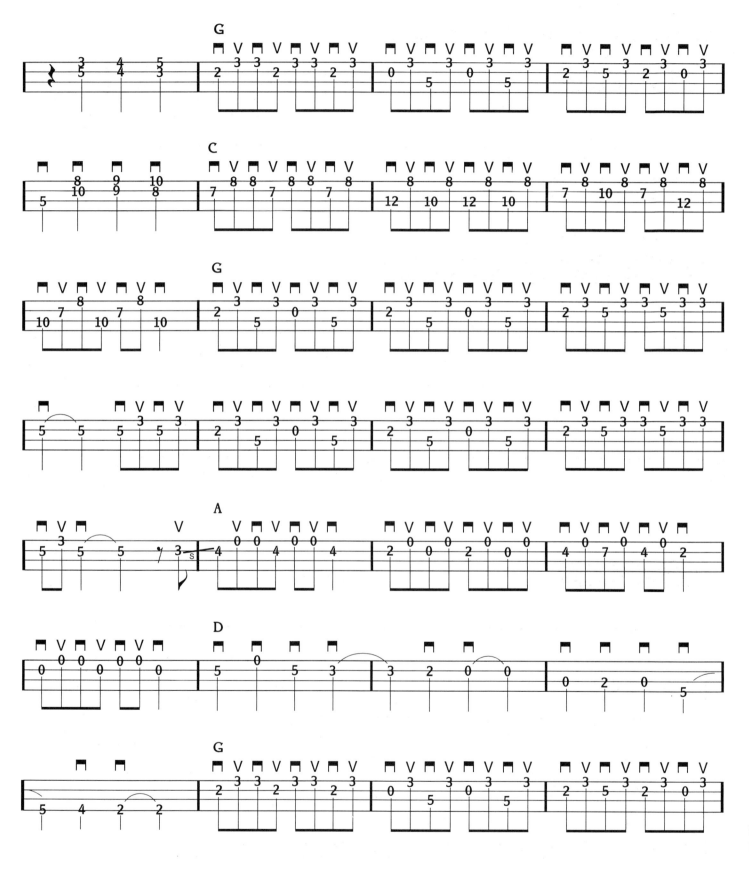

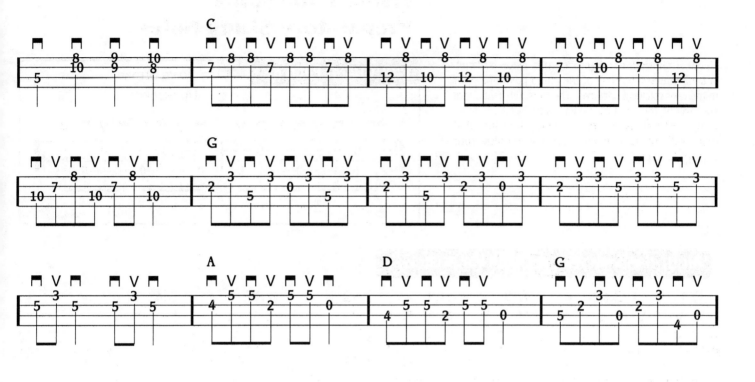

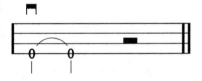

# Fisher's Hornpipe
# Preparatory Study Notes

**General Guidelines:** Approach this piece by familiarizing yourself with all of the chord positions prior to the crosspicking patterns. The most difficult chord shift will be the last two measures of Part A. By practicing these chord inversions, you will ensure that there will be no pauses when you employ your crosspicking patterns.

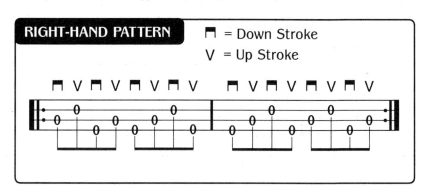

**RIGHT-HAND PATTERN**  ⊓ = Down Stroke  V = Up Stroke

**RIGHT-HAND PATTERN WITH CHORD EXERCISE**

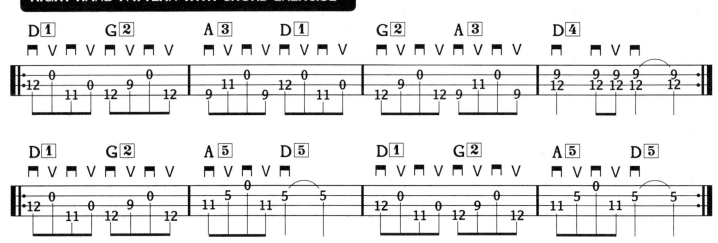

**CHORD POSITIONS**  (Numbers in square boxes correspond to positions used in chord exercise.)

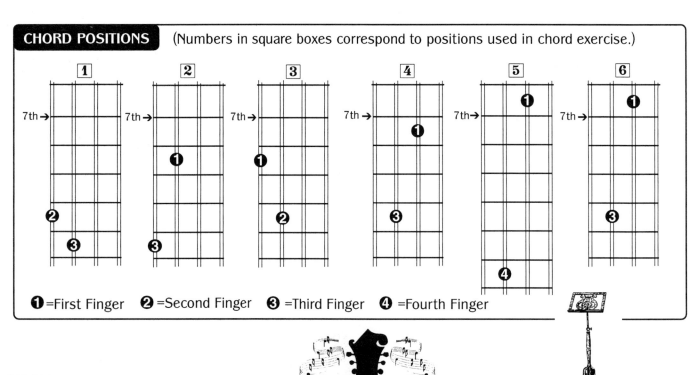

❶=First Finger  ❷=Second Finger  ❸=Third Finger  ❹=Fourth Finger

# Fisher's Hornpipe
# Preparatory Study Notes (cont.)

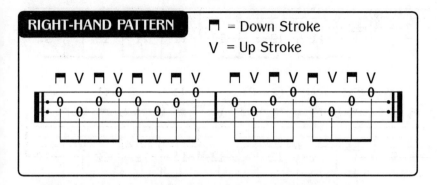

**RIGHT-HAND PATTERN**

⊓ = Down Stroke
V = Up Stroke

*Of Noted Interest:* This tune has been ascribed to an English composer named John Christian Fischer (1733-1800). Depending on the timing and accented notes, this tune can be played as a hoedown (as it is often played in the South), a reel (as played by fiddlers in New England) or a hornpipe.

**RIGHT-HAND PATTERN WITH CHORD EXERCISE**

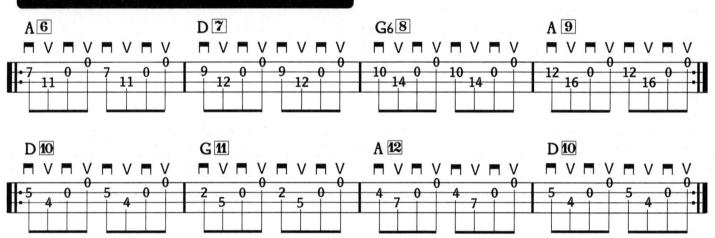

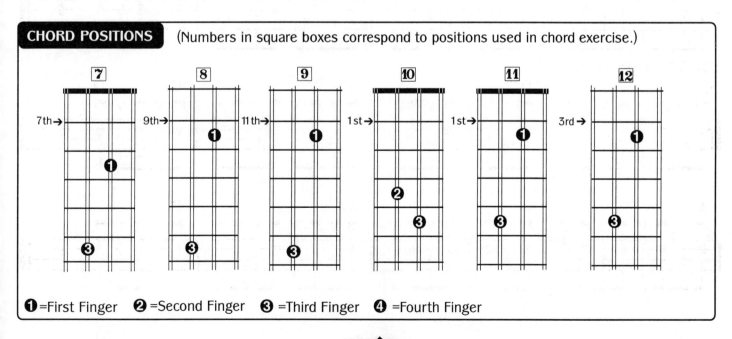

**CHORD POSITIONS** (Numbers in square boxes correspond to positions used in chord exercise.)

❶=First Finger   ❷=Second Finger   ❸=Third Finger   ❹=Fourth Finger

# Fisher's Hornpipe

Target Tempo:
♩ = 200

Key of D

Part A

Part B

Part B Variation

*Fiddle Style*

*Page 68.*

# PRACTICE NOTATION

# Eighth of January
# Preparatory Study Notes

*General Guidelines:* The approach to this melody is very fiddlistic in a melodic banjo sort of way. To try and capture every note of the melody, while still having the sustain of open strings to support it, was the objective. This approach can be applied effectively to all fiddle tunes. Experiment! Try adapting other fiddle tunes in the key of D utilizing some of the scales and passages illustrated in "Eight of January".

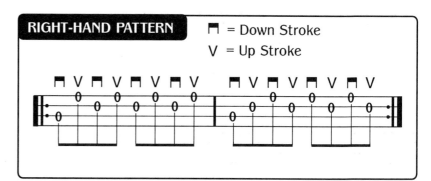

**RIGHT-HAND PATTERN**    ⊓ = Down Stroke
   V = Up Stroke

## RIGHT-HAND PATTERN WITH SCALE EXERCISE

**CHORD POSITIONS**    (Numbers in square boxes correspond to positions used in chord exercise.)

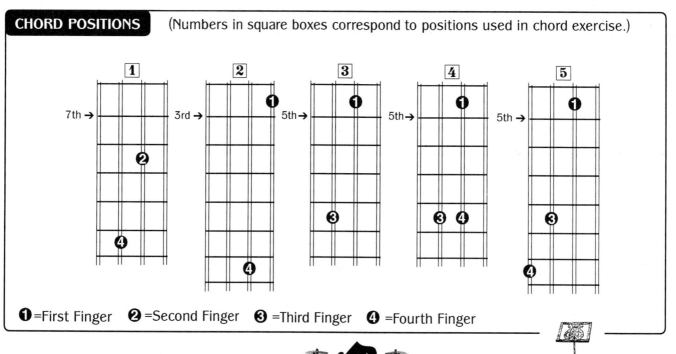

❶ =First Finger    ❷ =Second Finger    ❸ =Third Finger    ❹ =Fourth Finger

# Eighth of January
## Preparatory Study Notes (cont.)

**RIGHT-HAND PATTERN**

⊓ = Down Stroke
V = Up Stroke

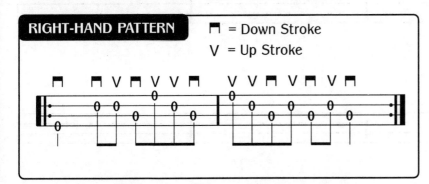

*Of Noted Interest:* Jimmy Driftwood had incorporated this melody into his famous composition "The Battle of New Orleans". The tune was written originally by frontier fiddlers in commemoration of the battle that took place in 1814. Because of Driftwood's songwriting efforts, everyone is familiar with this melody today.

**RIGHT-HAND PATTERN WITH CHORD EXERCISE**

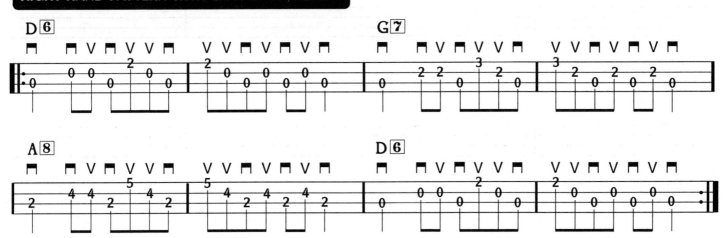

**CHORD POSITIONS** (Numbers in square boxes correspond to positions used in chord exercise.)

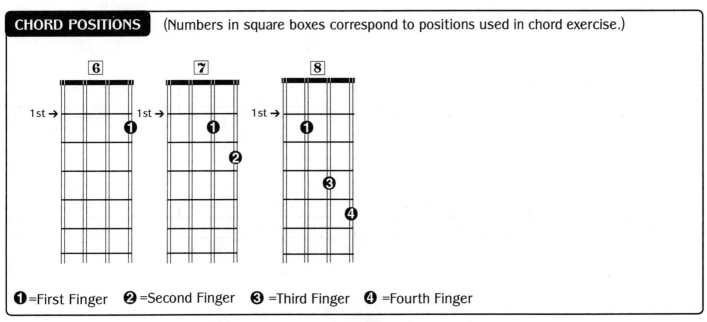

❶ =First Finger   ❷ =Second Finger   ❸ =Third Finger   ❹ =Fourth Finger

# Eighth of January

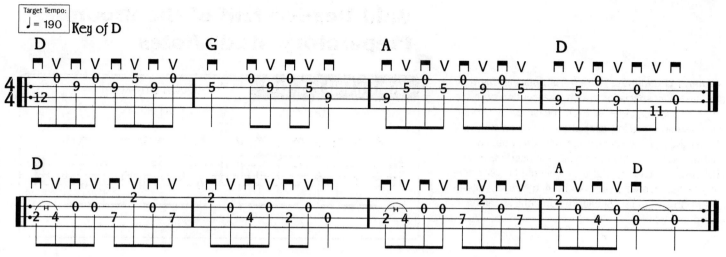

# Bald Headed End of the Broom
# Preparatory Study Notes

**General Guidelines:** Refrain from playing this tune too fast. Pay special attention to accenting both the first and fourth note of each measure. (Accenting only requires placing special emphasis on the note by playing it slightly louder than the other notes within the measure.) You'll notice, just as inflections in verbal communication, that a tune would be very boring to listen to if played without dynamics or accents—this would be similar to someone speaking in a monotonic voice.

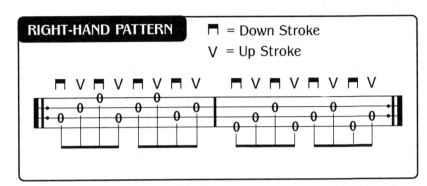

## RIGHT-HAND PATTERN WITH CHORD EXERCISE

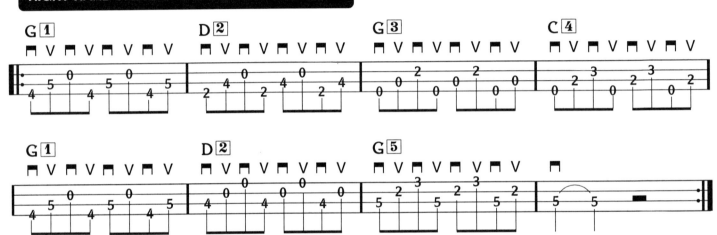

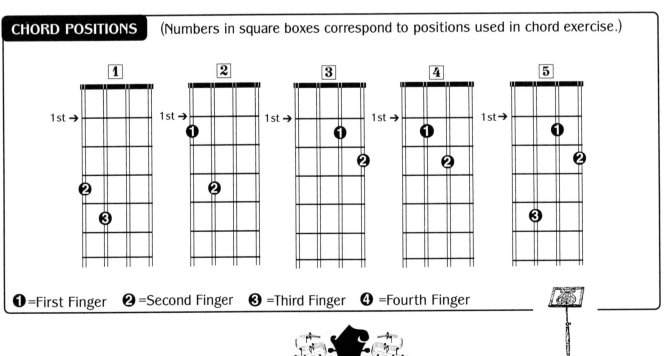

**❶=First Finger   ❷=Second Finger   ❸=Third Finger   ❹=Fourth Finger**

# Bald Headed End of the Broom
## Preparatory Study Notes (cont.)

**Of Noted Interest:** This fiddle tune is very reminiscent of the bluegrass standard "Eight more Miles to Louisville" written by Louis M. Jones. Check out Bud Orr's arrangement of this tune in his *Anthology of Mandolin Music*.

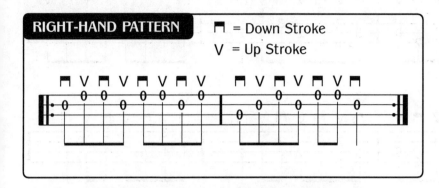

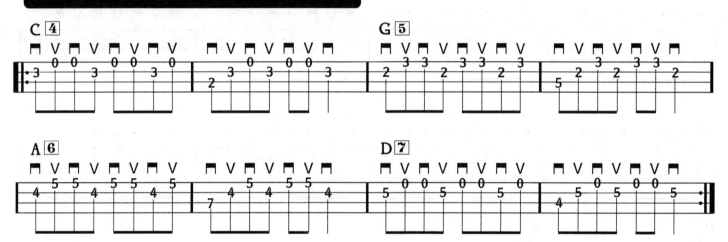

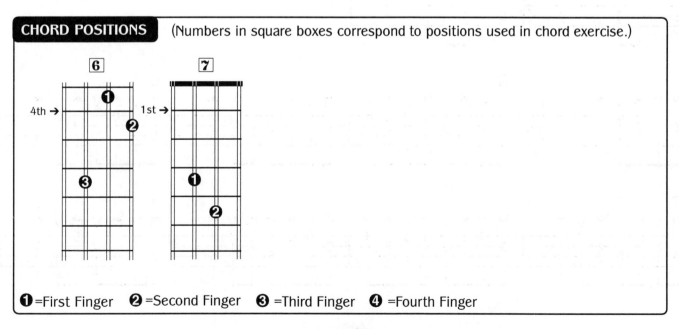

**❶** =First Finger   **❷** =Second Finger   **❸** =Third Finger   **❹** =Fourth Finger

# Bald Headed End of the Broom

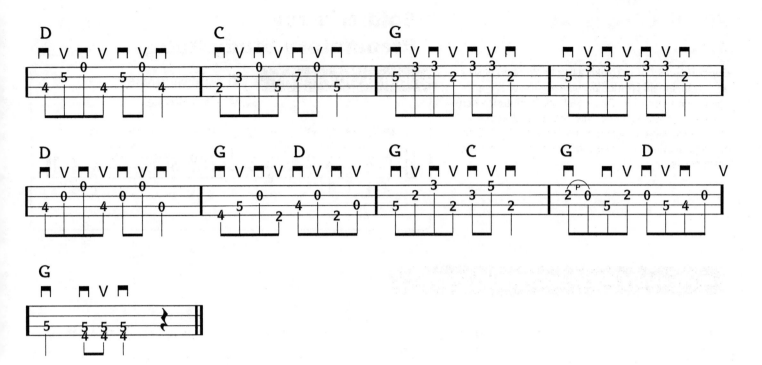

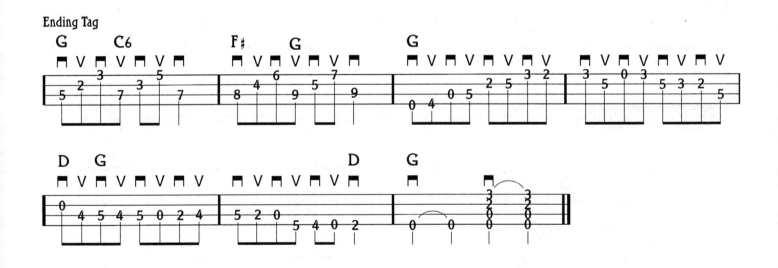

**Ending Tag**

# Soldier's Joy
# Preparatory Study Notes

*General Guidelines:* Think frailing banjo when playing this arrangement. Notice particularly the droning "A" open string in Part B. Be careful not to mute it when fretting adjacent strings. This drone is what flavors the tune similar to a frailing banjo. Focus on the difficult passage sections to ensure that you don't have any bottlenecks.

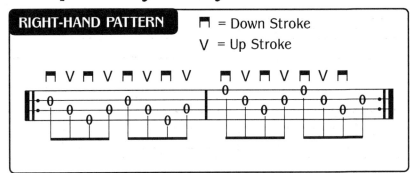

## RIGHT-HAND PATTERN WITH CHORD EXERCISE

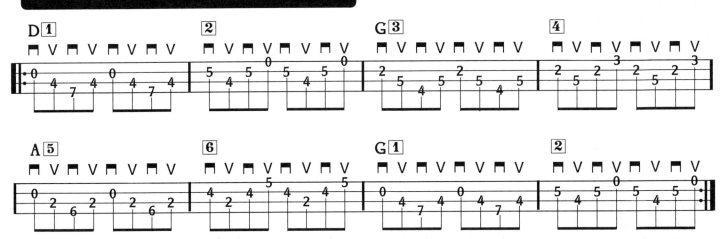

## CHORD POSITIONS  (Numbers in square boxes correspond to positions used in chord exercise.)

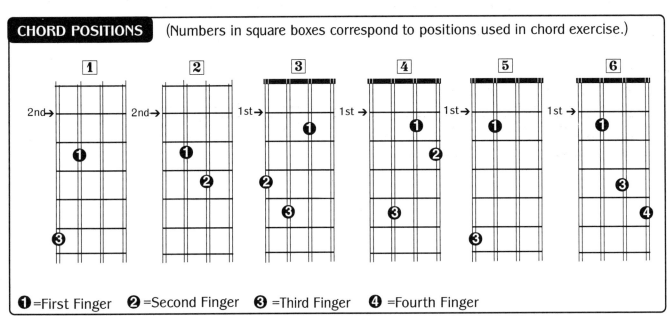

❶=First Finger  ❷=Second Finger  ❸=Third Finger  ❹=Fourth Finger

# Soldier's Joy
# Preparatory Study Notes (cont.)

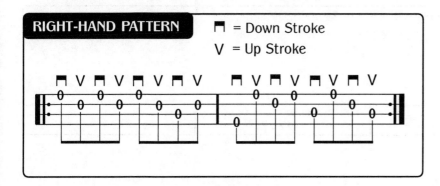

**RIGHT-HAND PATTERN**

$\sqcap$ = Down Stroke
V = Up Stroke

*General Guidelines:* One of my favorite versions of this tune is on the Nitty Gritty Dirt Band production *Will the Circle Be Unbroken* as a banjo duet with string bass backup. The following arrangement possesses similar overtones and sounds great unaccompanied.

**RIGHT-HAND PATTERN WITH CHORD EXERCISE**

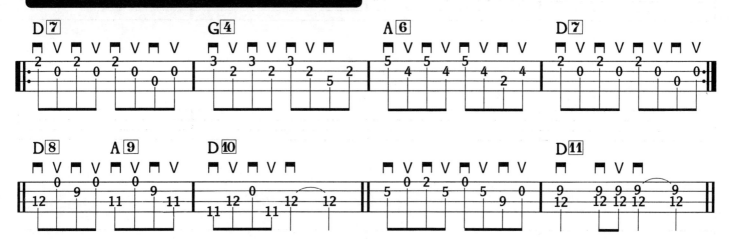

**CHORD POSITIONS** (Numbers in square boxes correspond to positions used in chord exercise.)

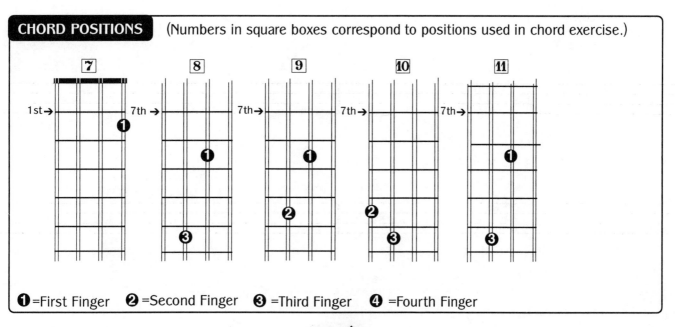

❶=First Finger  ❷=Second Finger  ❸=Third Finger  ❹=Fourth Finger

# PRACTICE NOTATION

# Soldier's Joy

# Blackberry Blossom
# Preparatory Study Notes

**General Guidelines:** Blackberry Blossom is normally played fast in a bluegrass setting. It happens to be a beautiful melody played fast or slow. This arrangement lends itself to be played at a medium pace. (Metronome Setting 190) This tune does require some rapid chord changes. Before attempting the exercises, try strumming the chords out at two beats per chord. This will establish left hand facility before trying to employ the intricacies of the crosspicking patterns.

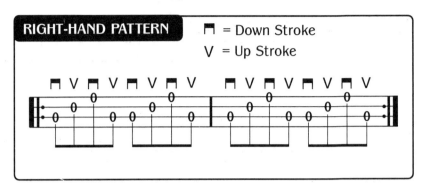

## RIGHT-HAND PATTERN WITH CHORD EXERCISE

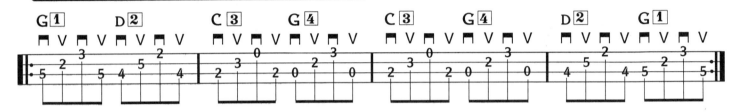

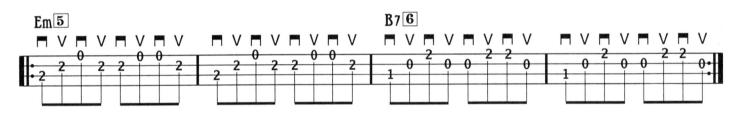

## CHORD POSITIONS (Numbers in square boxes correspond to positions used in chord exercise.)

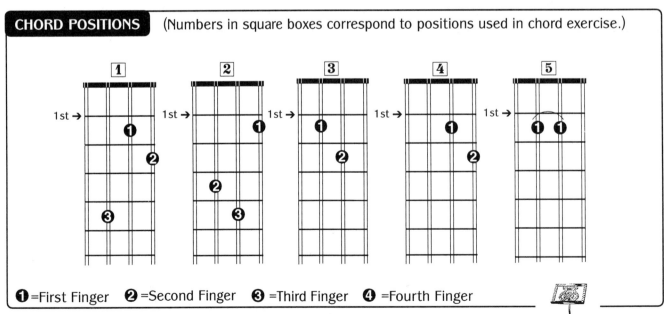

❶=First Finger  ❷=Second Finger  ❸=Third Finger  ❹=Fourth Finger

# Blackberry Blossom
# Preparatory Study Notes (cont.)

**RIGHT-HAND PATTERN**

⊓ = Down Stroke
V = Up Stroke

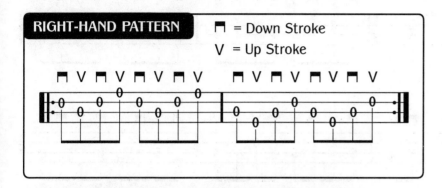

***Of Noted Interest:*** Even though it originated as a fiddle tune, this melody seems to have been written with melodic banjo in mind. Alan Munde does a great rendition of this on his tour de force *Banjo Sandwich*.

**RIGHT-HAND PATTERN WITH CHORD EXERCISE**

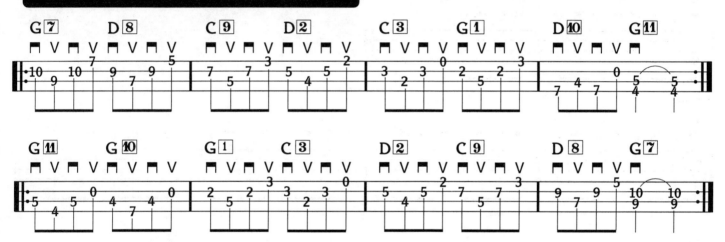

**CHORD POSITIONS** (Numbers in square boxes correspond to positions used in chord exercise.)

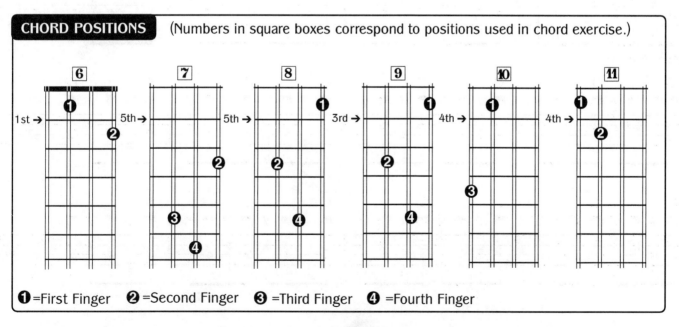

❶=First Finger ❷=Second Finger ❸=Third Finger ❹=Fourth Finger

# Blackberry Blossom

Target Tempo:
♩ = 190

Key of G

(Part A)

(Part B)

(Part A Variation)

*Fiddle Style*

*Page 84.*

# Whiskey Before Breakfast
# Preparatory Study Notes

*General Guidelines:* The melody is supported by the chords—notice that the low note of each chord gets the accent and carries the melody forward. Pay careful attention to the hammer-ons since they are an integral part of the melody. Make sure that your hammered on note rings true.

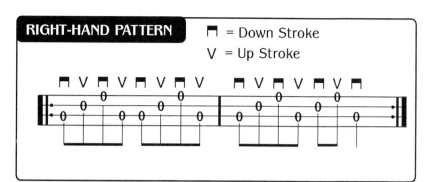

**RIGHT-HAND PATTERN WITH CHORD EXERCISE**

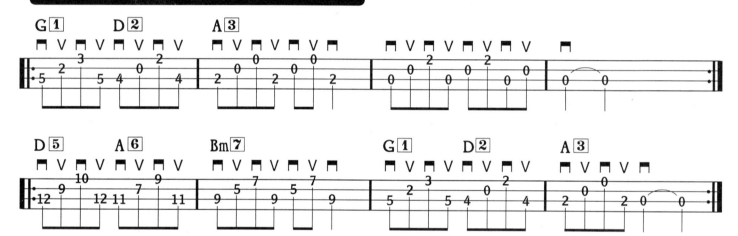

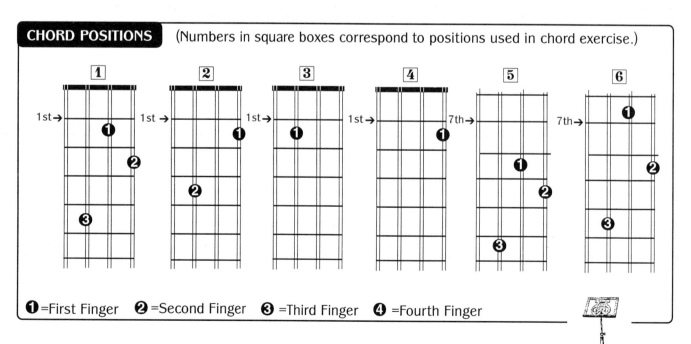

**❶**=First Finger   **❷**=Second Finger   **❸**=Third Finger   **❹**=Fourth Finger

# Whiskey Before Breakfast
# Preparatory Study Notes (cont.)

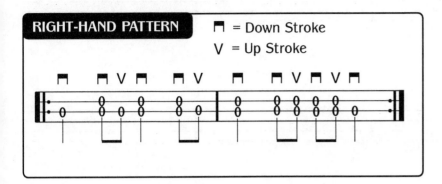

**Of Noted Interest:** Legend has it that this tune comes from the Canadian Maritime provinces where it is known as "The Spirits of Morning". The re-naming of the title probably went through the folk process where "Spirits" was interpreted as whiskey and "Morning" was associated with breakfast—ergo, "Whiskey Before Breakfast".

## RIGHT-HAND PATTERN WITH CHORD EXERCISE

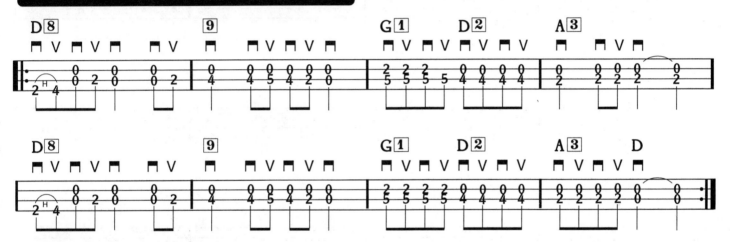

## FINGER POSITIONS (Numbers in square boxes correspond to positions used in chord exercise.)

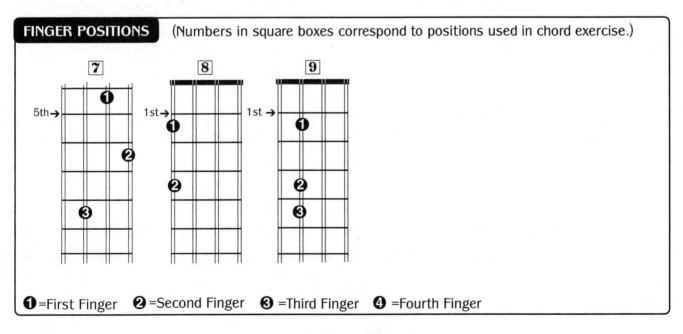

❶=First Finger  ❷=Second Finger  ❸=Third Finger  ❹=Fourth Finger

# PRACTICE NOTATION

# Whiskey Before Breakfast

Target Tempo:
♩ = 200

Key of D

**F-5 Lloyd Loar**

# Crosspicking Classical Style

## Greensleeves

## Ode To Joy

## Malagueña

# Greensleeves
# Preparatory Study Notes

**General Guidelines:** This melody is normally played in 3/4 time. Our arrangement, adapted to crosspicking, is written in 4/4 time and is played slightly faster than what is expected. As a variation, try playing this melody slowly in 3/4 time and then jumping into the 4/4 crosspicking arrangement. It will add the surprise element to your performance and may even keep your audience from nodding off.

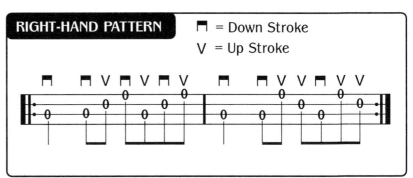

**RIGHT-HAND PATTERN**

⊓ = Down Stroke
V = Up Stroke

## RIGHT-HAND PATTERN WITH CHORD EXERCISE

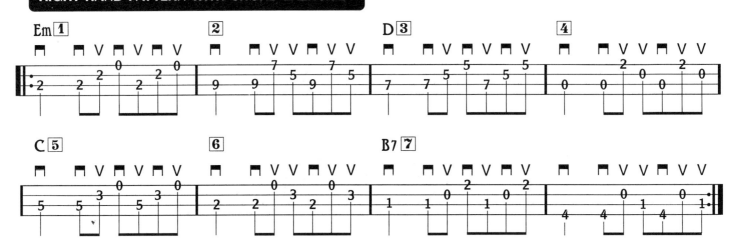

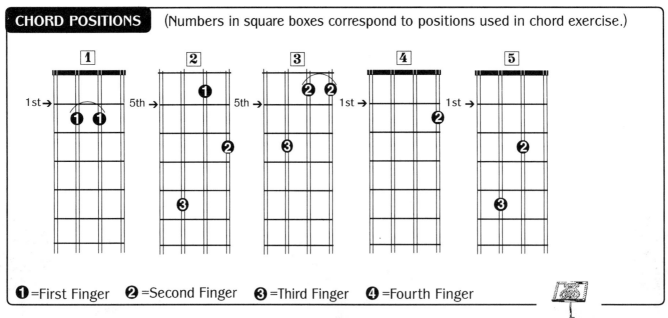

**CHORD POSITIONS**  (Numbers in square boxes correspond to positions used in chord exercise.)

❶=First Finger  ❷=Second Finger  ❸=Third Finger  ❹=Fourth Finger

# Greensleeves
## Preparatory Study Notes (cont.)

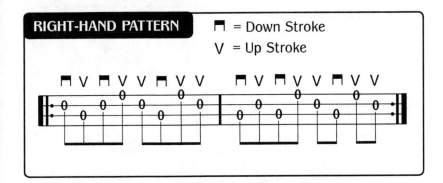

**RIGHT-HAND PATTERN**

⊓ = Down Stroke

V = Up Stroke

***General Guidelines:*** This melody has been ascribed to King Henry the VIII–no doubt, it's centuries old yet, nonetheless, defeats time.

**RIGHT-HAND PATTERN WITH CHORD EXERCISE**

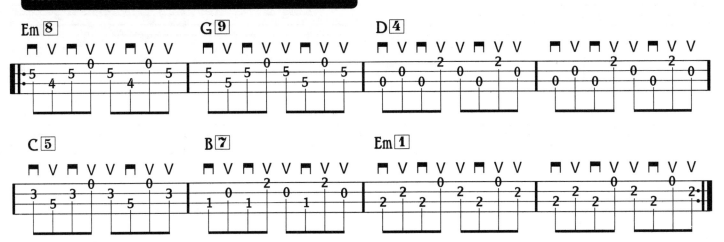

**CHORD POSITIONS** (Numbers in square boxes correspond to positions used in chord exercise.)

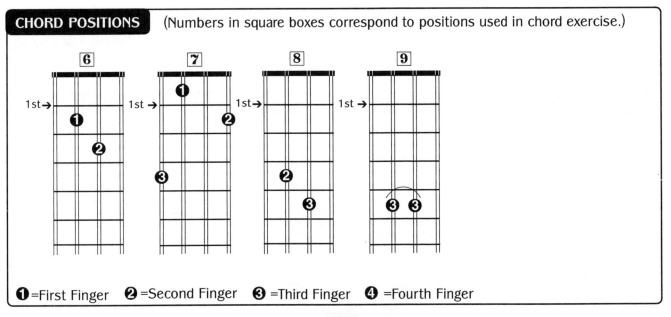

❶ =First Finger  ❷ =Second Finger  ❸ =Third Finger  ❹ =Fourth Finger

# Greensleeves

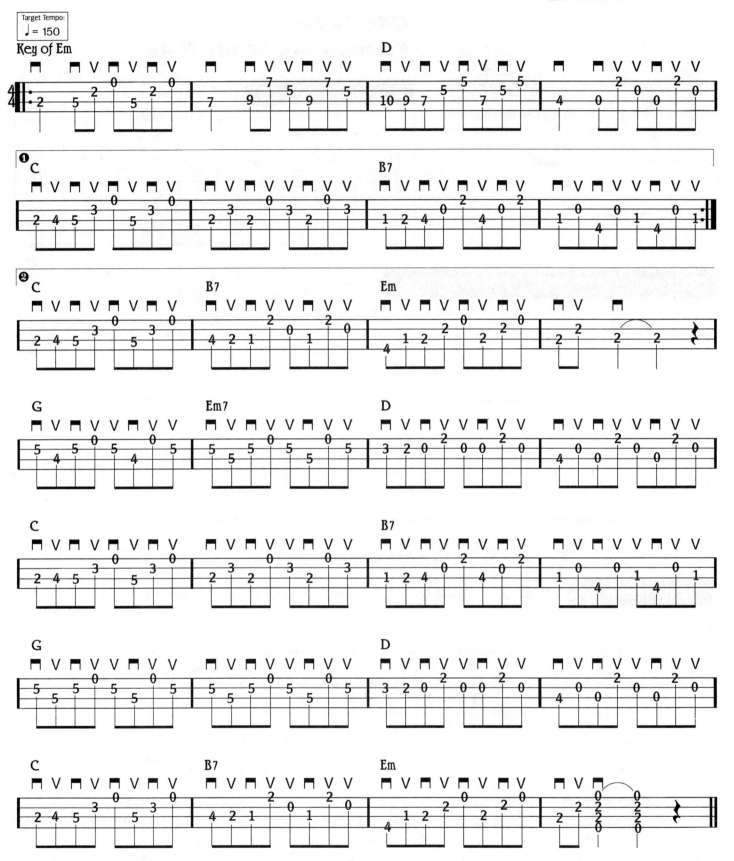

# Ode to Joy
# Preparatory Study Notes

*General Guidelines:* In this arrangement, drone notes are being played throughout the piece. The crosspicking pattern follows the alternating bass variation. You may vary your accents by placing them on either the melody notes or the drone notes. This piece makes for an excellent right hand workout.

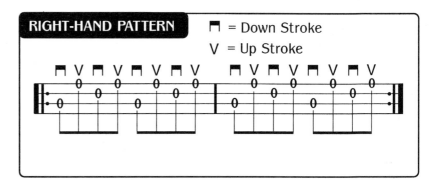

## RIGHT-HAND PATTERN WITH CHORD EXERCISE

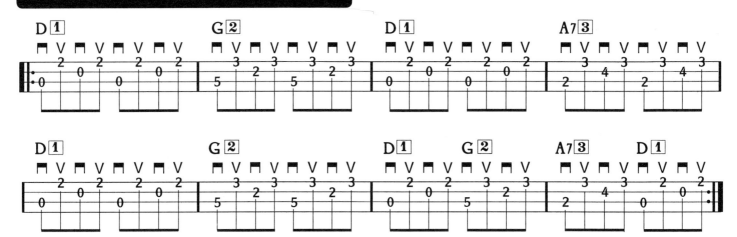

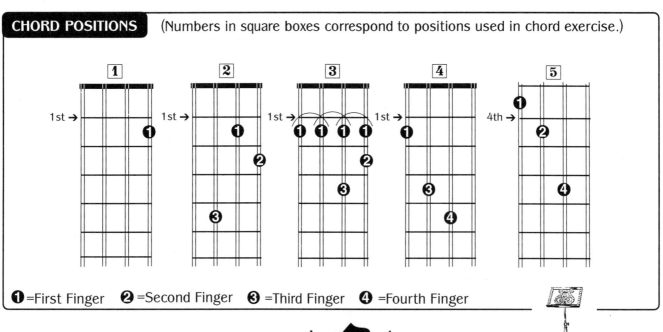

❶=First Finger   ❷=Second Finger   ❸=Third Finger   ❹=Fourth Finger

# Ode to Joy
# Preparatory Study Notes (cont.)

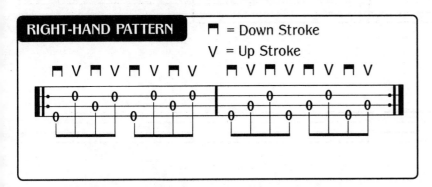

**RIGHT-HAND PATTERN**

⊓ = Down Stroke

V = Up Stroke

*Of Noted Interest:* Also known as "Beethoven's Ninth", or "Beethoven's Chorale", this interpretation has a very improvisatory feel. Timing is not critical; you may speed it up or slow it down in parts without sacrificing the mood of the piece. The melody is simple but persuasive.

**RIGHT-HAND PATTERN WITH CHORD EXERCISE**

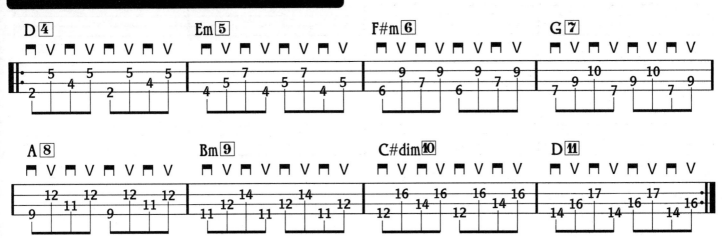

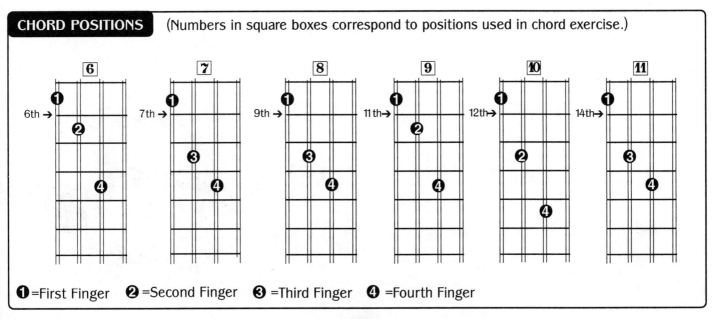

**CHORD POSITIONS**    (Numbers in square boxes correspond to positions used in chord exercise.)

❶=First Finger   ❷=Second Finger   ❸=Third Finger   ❹=Fourth Finger

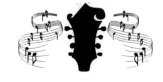

# Ode to Joy

(Beethoven)

Target Tempo:
♩ = 170

Key of D

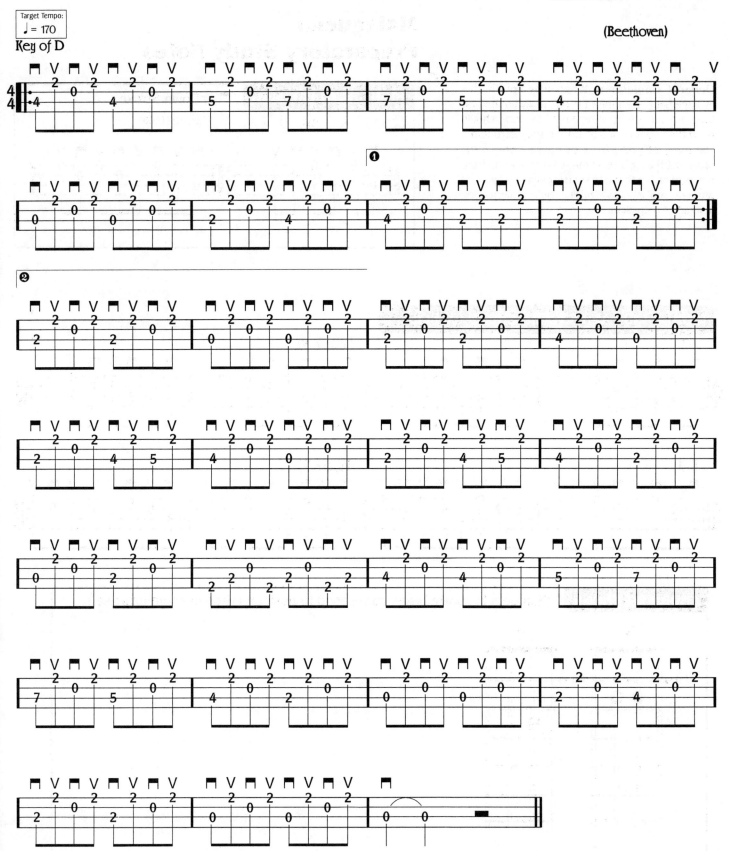

# Malagueña
# Preparatory Study Notes

*General Guidelines*: When attempting this arrangement, start the tune off slowly on the first time around. The final repeat of the tune should be at the target tempo of 180 on the metronome. The most difficult part of this piece involves the span that the right hand must make to jump from the third string to the first string—if accomplished properly, you should sound like you're fingerpicking instead of flatpicking.

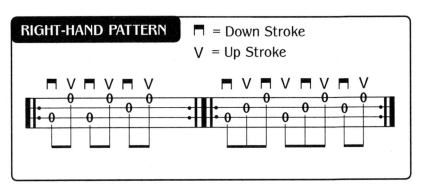

**RIGHT-HAND PATTERN WITH CHORD EXERCISE**

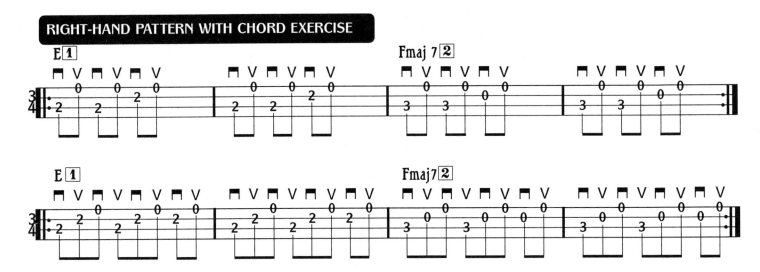

**CHORD POSITIONS** (Numbers in square boxes correspond to positions used in chord exercise.)

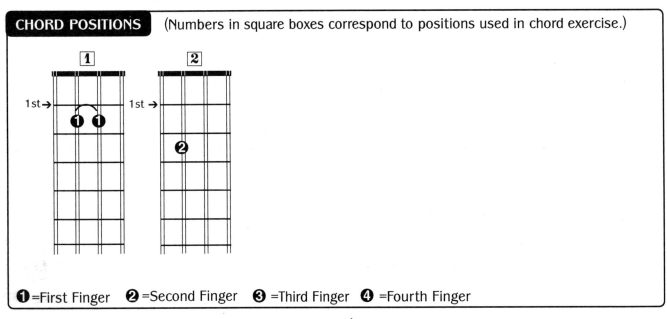

❶=First Finger ❷=Second Finger ❸=Third Finger ❹=Fourth Finger

# Malagueña
# Preparatory Study Notes (cont.)

*Of Noted Interest:* You've heard flamenco guitar—now we have flamenco mandolin. Malagueña is in triple-time based on a dance from Malaga Spain. This tune just touches on the many possibilities crosspicking offers in a flamenco vein.

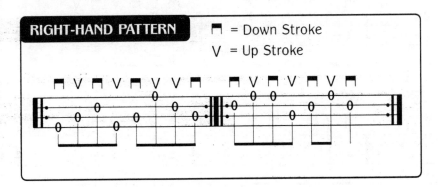

## RIGHT-HAND PATTERN WITH CHORD EXERCISE

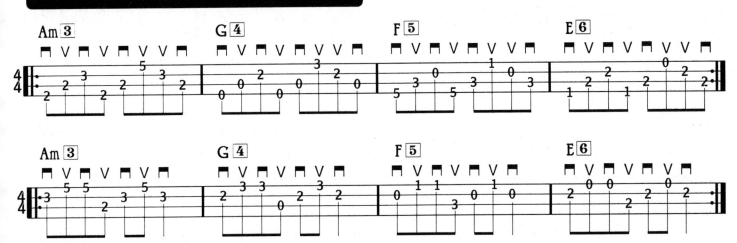

## CHORD POSITIONS

(Numbers in square boxes correspond to positions used in chord exercise.)

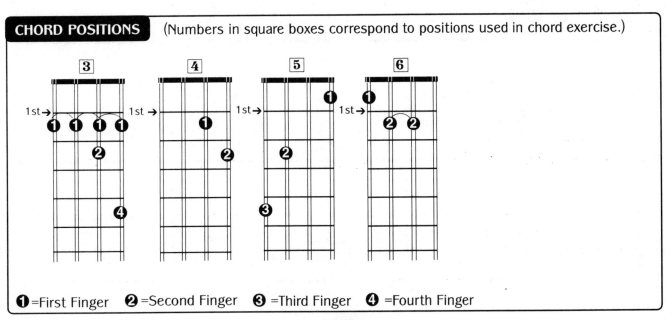

❶=First Finger  ❷=Second Finger  ❸=Third Finger  ❹=Fourth Finger

# Malagueña
# (A Spanish Study)

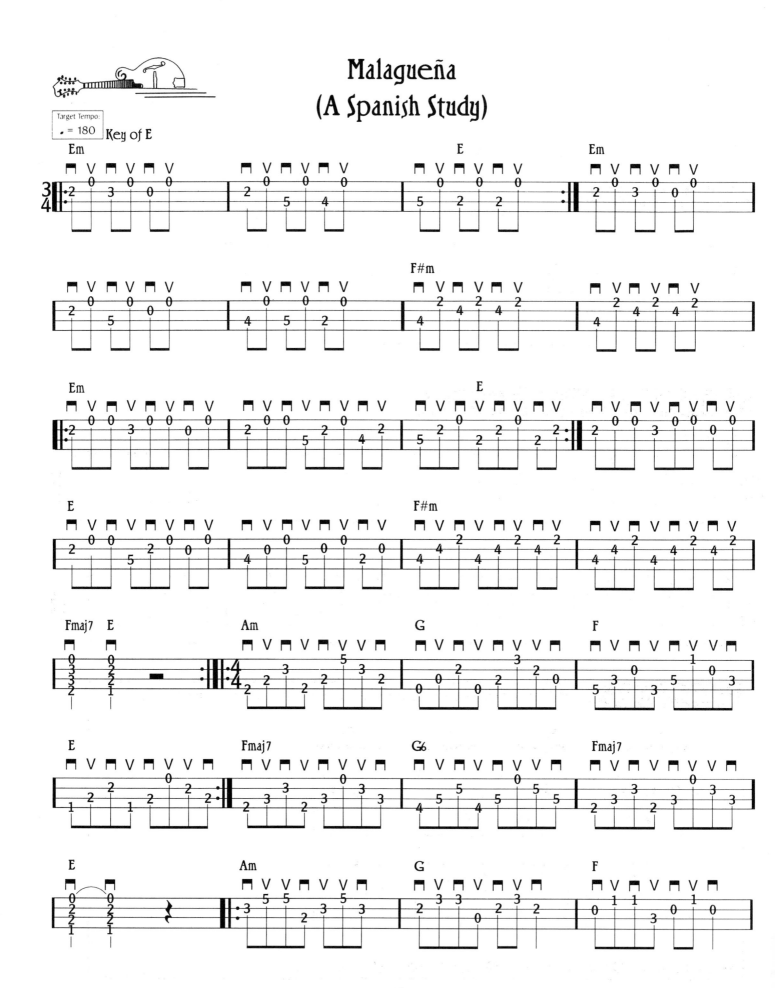

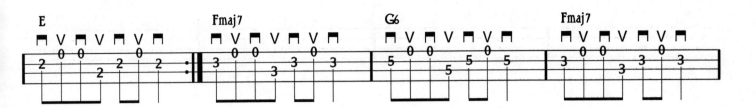

# Crosspicking Jazz/Ragtime Style

## Dill Pickle Rag

## Beaumont Rag

## Cotton Patch Rag

# Dill Pickle Rag
# Preparatory Study Notes

**General Guidelines:** Experiment by interchanging the chord exercises with the original piece. Make sure that you're fitting them into the same chordal phrases. You might also want to try plugging in other patterns over these same chord positions. Play this tune with the classic ragtime feel by accenting the first and third notes of each measure.

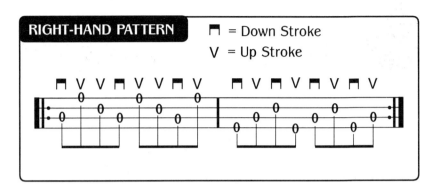

**RIGHT-HAND PATTERN WITH CHORD EXERCISE**

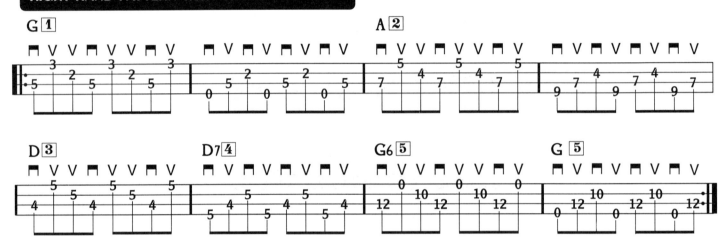

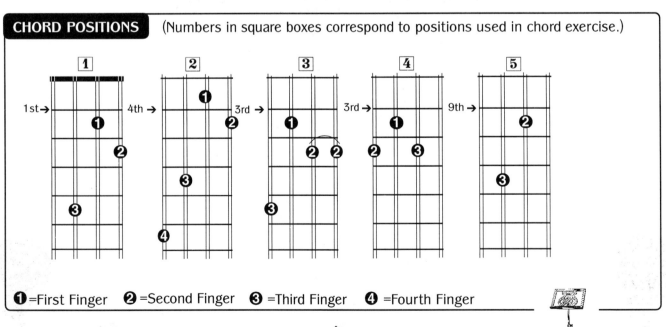

**CHORD POSITIONS** (Numbers in square boxes correspond to positions used in chord exercise.)

❶=First Finger  ❷=Second Finger  ❸=Third Finger  ❹=Fourth Finger

# Dill Pickle Rag
## Preparatory Study Notes (cont.)

**RIGHT-HAND PATTERN**

⊓ = Down Stroke

V = Up Stroke

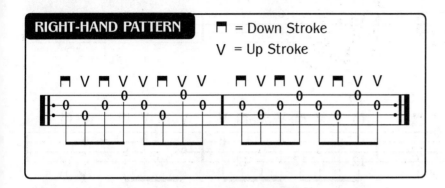

*Of Noted Interest:* As is true of most other ragtime tunes, "Dill Pickle Rag" was originally written on piano. Play it at a moderate ragtime pace with a syncopated feel.

**RIGHT-HAND PATTERN WITH CHORD EXERCISE**

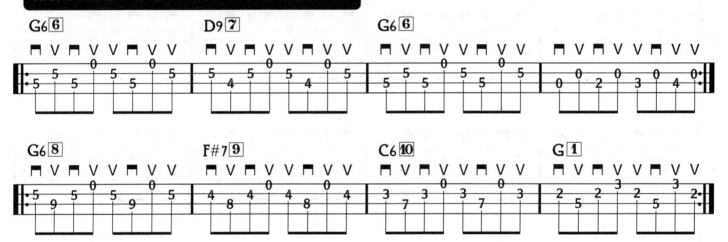

**CHORD POSITIONS** (Numbers in square boxes correspond to positions used in chord exercise.)

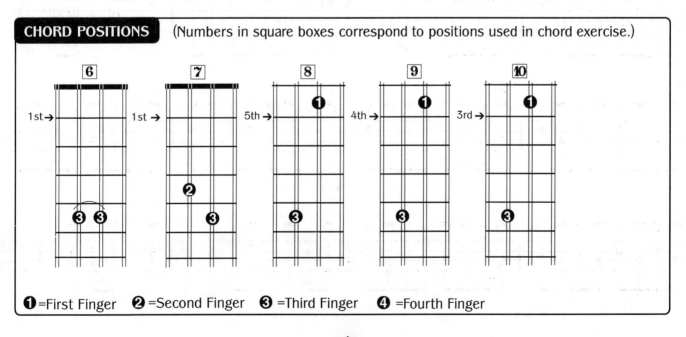

❶=First Finger  ❷=Second Finger  ❸=Third Finger  ❹=Fourth Finger

# Dill Pickle Rag

(C.L. Johnson)

Target Tempo:
♩ = 200

Key of G

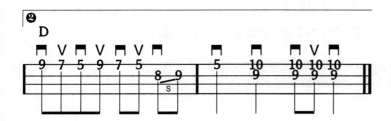

**②** D

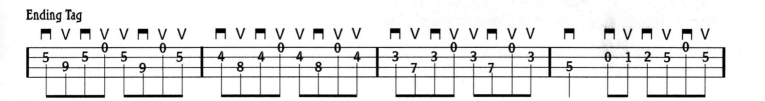

**Ending Tag**

# Beaumont Rag
# Preparatory Study Notes

*General Guidelines:* The A part is played in a melodic banjo fashion. This approach involves playing the melody without attacking the same string twice. Try taking melodies you're familiar with and creating your own melodic banjo arrangements on mandolin.

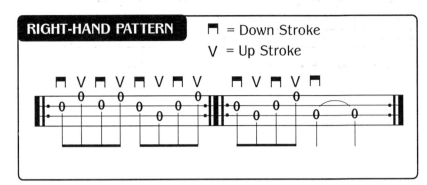

**RIGHT-HAND PATTERN**  ⊓ = Down Stroke   V = Up Stroke

## RIGHT-HAND PATTERN WITH CHORD EXERCISE

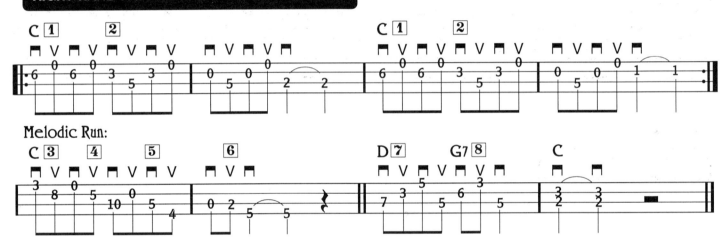

Melodic Run:

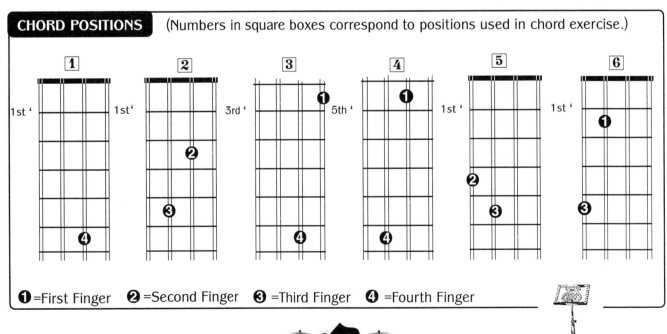

**CHORD POSITIONS**   (Numbers in square boxes correspond to positions used in chord exercise.)

❶=First Finger   ❷=Second Finger   ❸=Third Finger   ❹=Fourth Finger

# Beaumont Rag
# Preparatory Study Notes (cont.)

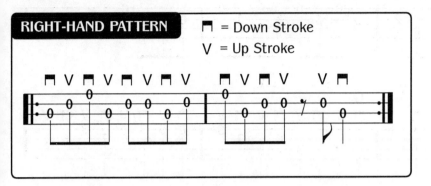

**RIGHT-HAND PATTERN**

⊓ = Down Stroke
V = Up Stroke

*Of Noted Interest:* A Texas-Style fiddle tune with a ragtime syncopation, made popular by artists such as Doc Watson & Dan Crary. Ray Valla has an excellent arrangement of this piece in his *Deluxe Bluegrass Mandolin Method.*

**RIGHT-HAND PATTERN WITH CHORD EXERCISE**

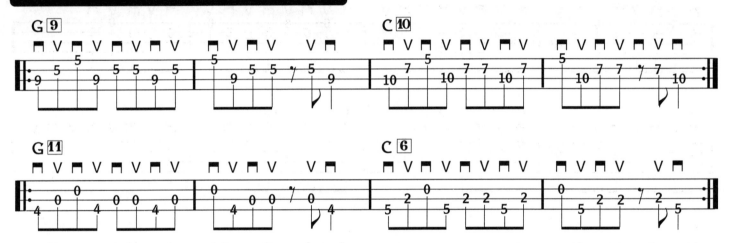

**CHORD POSITIONS** (Numbers in square boxes correspond to positions used in chord exercise.)

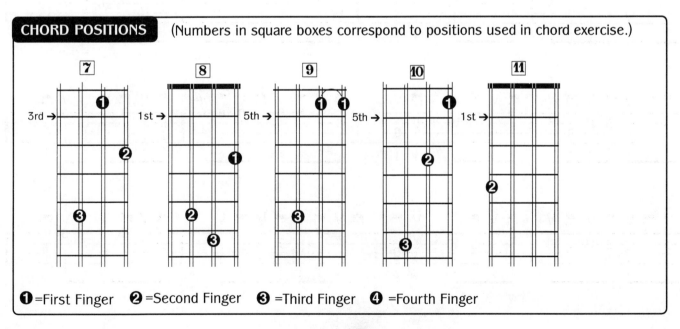

❶=First Finger  ❷=Second Finger  ❸=Third Finger  ❹=Fourth Finger

# Beaumont Rag

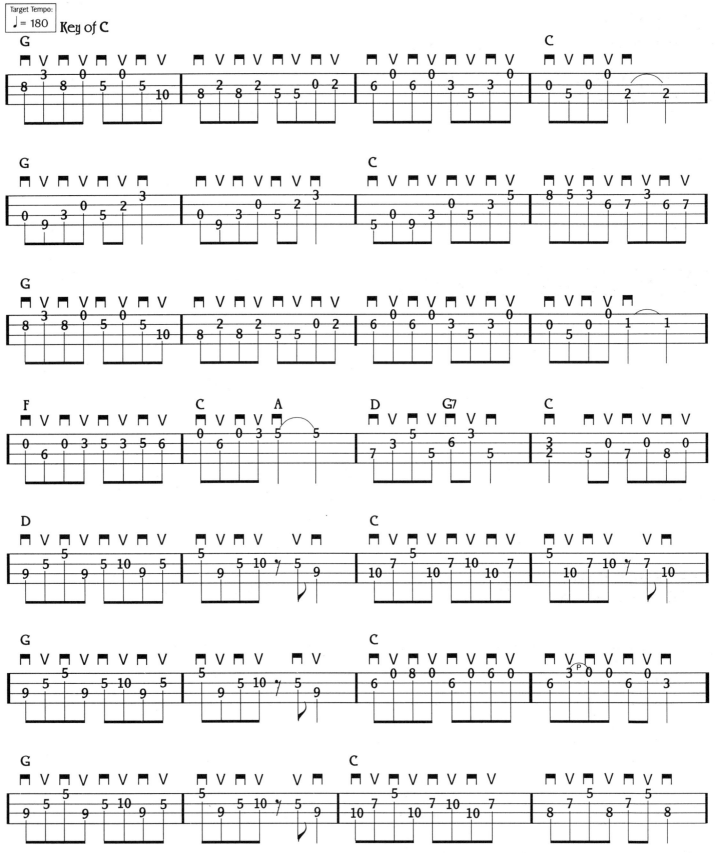

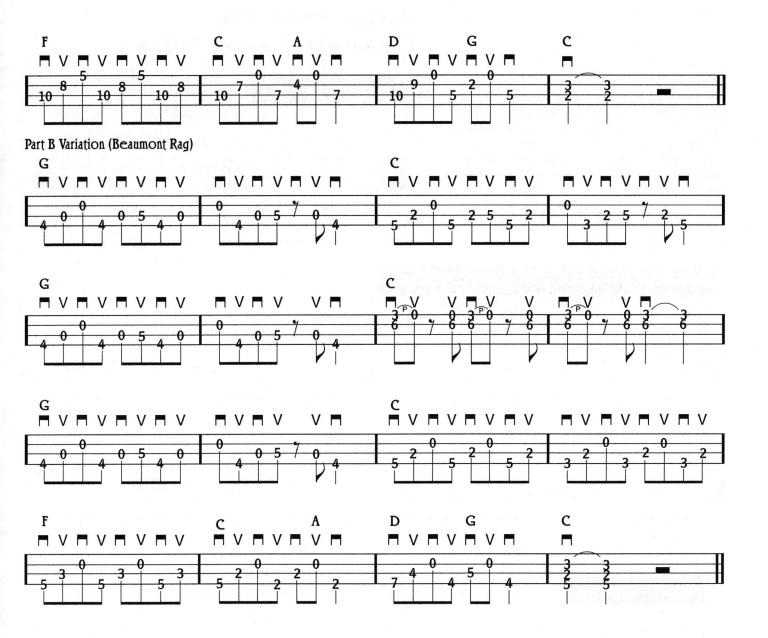

**Part B Variation (Beaumont Rag)**

# Cotton Patch Rag
# Preparatory Study Notes

**General Guidelines:** The most challenging part of this tune is the impossible finger stretches. You'll be spanning 8 frets with one hand. After accomplishing this piece, you'll be well on your way to becoming a crosspicking master mandolinist. Be sure you're completely comfortable with the exercises before attempting to play the tune. There should be no pauses between the changes.

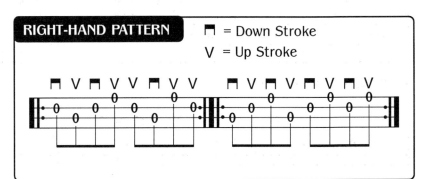

**RIGHT-HAND PATTERN WITH CHORD EXERCISE**

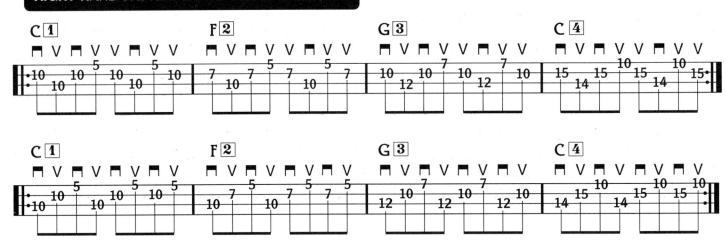

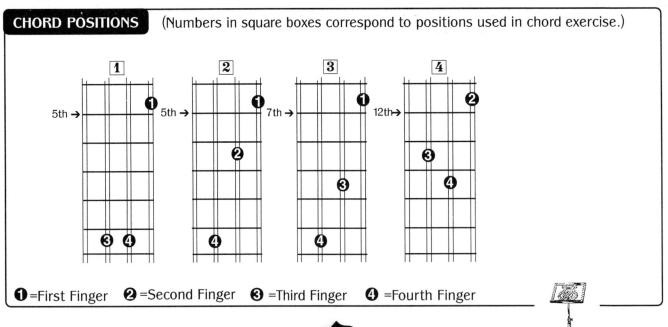

**❶** =First Finger    **❷** =Second Finger    **❸** =Third Finger    **❹** =Fourth Finger

# Cotton Patch Rag
## Preparatory Study Notes (cont.)

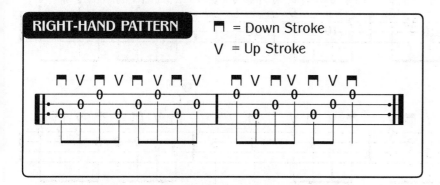

**RIGHT-HAND PATTERN**

∏ = Down Stroke
V = Up Stroke

*Of Noted Interest:* A popular Texas-Style Fiddle tune, even Tiny Moore, mandolinist for Bob Willis & His Texas Playboys, played this one!

**RIGHT-HAND PATTERN WITH CHORD EXERCISE**

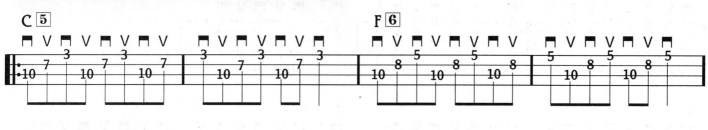

**CHORD POSITIONS**  (Numbers in square boxes correspond to positions used in chord exercise.)

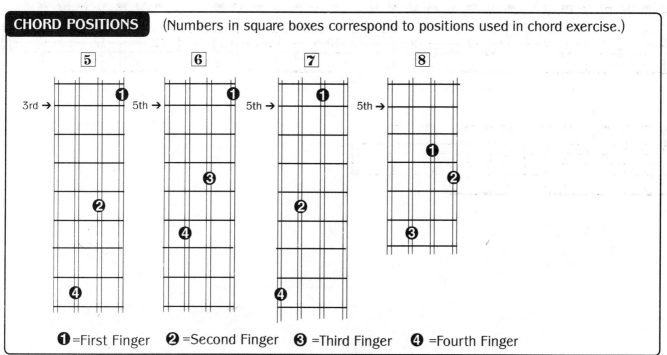

❶=First Finger   ❷=Second Finger   ❸=Third Finger   ❹=Fourth Finger

# Cotton Patch Rag

Target Tempo:
♩ = 200

Key of C

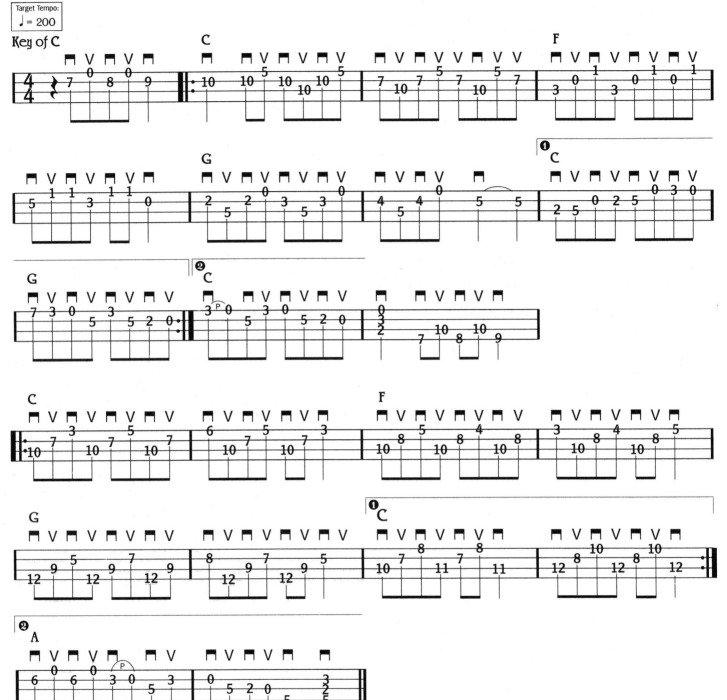

# Conclusion

The many crosspicking tunes and exercises you've learned should give you a jumping-off point for developing many other possibilities; these innovations can only be accomplished through your unique musical perspective. Experiment! Try applying the many rolls and patterns to other melodies. When playing behind vocalists or instrumentalists, try some crosspicking patterns as backup variations. Listen to other mandolinists with an assiduous ear. Many mandolin masters have employed crosspicking, although some only minutely, in their playing: David Grisman, Doyle Lawson, John McEuen, Sam Bush, Jimmy Gaudreau are only a few of the many. The most outstanding crosspicking exponent, who has left a legacy of crosspicking tunes from the 1950s to today, is Jesse McReynolds. Buy every recording of Jesse's that you can get your hands on. Jesse has taken crosspicking into new dimensions for decades. He infuses crosspicking with an air of elegance yet to be matched.

Everyone has their own musical journey. No two musicians have ever followed the exact same path. We are all a culmination of the listening influences and music books we've studied. Just like a painting, a song is interpreted differently by every musician that performs it. Even if the notes are played exactly in the same place, so many other shades of difference come into play. For instance: the volume, the attack, the medium utilized (type of strings, picks or instrument), the feel, and many other nuances will affect the outcome of the interpreted piece. So, discover your own journey and remember, be as it may, there is no such thing as being a mirror image of another musician.

Don't stop learning! The journey only begins where you've left off.

# A Selection of Suggested Listening

*A sampling of my personal favorites. Many of these recordings may no longer be available. Although, they may soon be reissued on CD.*

| ARTIST | RECORDING | RECORD LABEL |
|---|---|---|
| **Norman Blake** | *Whiskey Before Breakfast* | Rounder Records |
| | *Back Home in Sulphur Springs* | Rounder Records |
| | *Slow Train Through Georgia* | Rounder Records |
| | *Full Moon on the Farm* | Rounder Records |
| | *Lighthouse on the Shore* | Rounder Records |
| | *Nashville Blues* | Rounder Records |
| | *Original Underground Music from the Mysterious South* | Rounder Records |
| | *Just Gimme Somethin' I'm Used To* | Shanachie Records |
| with Nancy Blake | *Blind Dog* | Rounder Records |
| | *Natasha's Waltz* | Rounder Records |
| | *The Norman and Nancy Blake Compact Disc* | Rounder Records |
| with Red Rector | *Norman Blake & Red Rector* | County |
| with Jethro Burns | *Jethro Burns, Norman Blake Sam Bush, Tut Taylor* | Flying Fish |
| **Sam Bush** | *Late As Usual* | Rounder Records |
| | *Glamour and Grits* | Sugar Hill Records |
| with New Grass Revival | *New Grass Revival* | Starday |
| | *When the Storm is Over* | Flying Fish Records |
| | *Fly Through the Country* | Flying Fish Records |
| | *Too Late to Turn Back Now* | Flying Fish Records |
| | *The Festival Tapes* | Flying Fish Records |
| | *Barren County* | Flying Fish Records |
| | *Commonwealth* | Flying Fish Records |
| | *On the Boulevard* | Sugar Hill Records |
| | *New Grass Revival* | EMI America |
| | *Hold to a Dream* | EMI America |
| | *Friday Night in America* | EMI America |
| with Alan Munde | *Poor Richard's Almanac* | American Heritage |
| | *Sam and Alan Together Again For The First Time* | Ridge Runner |

# A Selection of Suggested Listening

| ARTIST | RECORDING | RECORD LABEL |
|---|---|---|
| **Sam Bush** (cont.)<br>with Jerry Douglas | *Under the Wire*<br>*Everything Is Gonna Work Out Fine* | MCA<br>Rounder |
| **Jimmy Gaudreau** | *The Gaudreau Mandolin Album* | Puritan Records |
| **David Grisman**<br><br><br><br><br><br><br><br><br>with Old and In the Way<br><br><br>with Tony Rice | *The David Grisman Quintet*<br>*Early Dawg*<br>*The David Grisman*<br>*       Rounder Compact Disc*<br>*The David Grisman Quintet*<br>*       Quintet '80*<br>*Hot Dawg*<br>*Mando Mondo*<br><br>*Old and In the Way*<br>*That High Lone Sound - Vol. 1*<br><br>*Tone Poems* | Rhino Records<br>Sugar Hill Records<br><br>Rounder Records<br><br>Warner Bros.<br>Horizon Music<br>        Warner Bros.<br><br>Rounder Records<br>Acoustic Disc<br><br>Acoustic Disc |
| **Doyle Lawson** | *Tennessee Dream* | County |
| **Dave Martini** | *Mr. Mandolin Man*<br>*Mr. Mandolin Man Picks Again*<br>*Sounds of the Mandolin Man* | Stoneway STY 126<br>Stoneway STY 134<br>Stoneway STY 174 |
| **Jesse McReynolds**<br>with Jim & Jesse<br><br><br><br><br><br>with Allen Shelton | *Airmail Special*<br>*Mandolin Workshop*<br>*The Jim & Jesse Story*<br>*Epic Bluegrass Hits*<br>*In The Tradition*<br>*Music Among Friends*<br><br>*Shelton Special* | Rebel Records<br>Hilltop<br>CMH<br>Rounder Records<br>Rounder Records<br>Rounder Records<br><br>Rounder Records |

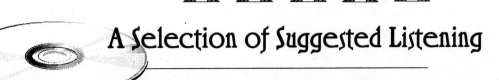

# A Selection of Suggested Listening

| ARTIST | RECORDING | RECORD LABEL |
|---|---|---|
| **Steve Smith** | *Distant Lands* <br> *Other Places, Times & Lives* | Desert Night Music <br> Desert Night Music |
| **Andy Statman** <br> with Country Cooking | *Country Cooking* <br> *26 Bluegrass Originals* | Rounder Records <br> Rounder Records |
| **Roland White** | *Appalachian Swing!* <br> *Kentucky Colonels: 1965-67* | Rounder Records <br> Rounder Records |
| **Nitty Gritty Dirt Band** | *Will the Circle be Unbroken* | Liberty Records |

# A Selection for Further Study

Collecting and studying an extensive library of mandolin instruction material will assist you in future efforts of becoming an accomplished mandolinist. If you do not know how to read music, allow yourself the opportunity by acquiring the suggested study material included here. It will transform you into a well-rounded mandolinist and enable you to take on anything thrown your way. Consider also the importance of building a vast repertoire—by learning and memorizing many different songs, you'll be increasing your proficiency, knowledge of how songs are composed, ability to read tablature and standard notation, knowledge of chords and scales, along with possessing a selection of tunes that will fill any request.

Some of the books listed may be out of print. They are all included since many books fall in and out of print periodically. These books fall into many categories; the main division would be that some are methodology books, while others are songbooks. A methodology book instructs on how to approach the instrument in an effort to build technique; a songbook is more of a repository—a collection of songs that will build your repertoire.

## BLUEGRASS & FOLK INSTRUCTION

### I. Backporch Flatpicking for Mandolin & Guitar

Sara Johnson & Maynard Johnson
©1977 • Saginaw River Music, Limited
**Type:** Songbook
**Level:** Beginner/Intermediate
**Number of Pages:** 88
**Notation:** Standard/Tablature
Mainly a songbook, it also includes some basic technique instructions. The pieces are all traditional fiddle tunes.

### II. How to Play Mandolin

Jack Tottle
©1977 • Acorn Music Press
**Type:** Methodology
**Level:** Beginner
**Number of Pages:** 64
**Notation:** Standard/Tablature
A method book that includes some folk tunes, bluegrass standards and even a couple of Beatle tunes. Includes a concise chord dictionary for reference.

### III. The Bluegrass Mandolin Player's Song Book

Frank Javorsek
©1978 • Ryckman & Beck Music Publishing
**Type:** Songbook
**Level:** Beginner/Intermediate
**Number of Pages:** 78
**Notation:** Standard/Tablature
A collection of bluegrass songs that every bluegrass mandolin player should know. Some basic technique is also covered.

### IV. Merlin's Magical Mandolin Method

Joe Carr
©1978 • Bluegrass Tabs
**Type:** Songbook
**Level:** Intermediate/Advanced
**Number of Pages:** 26
**Notation:** Tablature
A collection of bluegrass songs that include arrangements the author recorded with the Country Gazette. There are no time signatures so it's required to listen to the tunes on the accompanying tape before attempting to learn them.

# A Selection for Further Study

## BLUEGRASS & FOLK INSTRUCTION (cont.)

### V. Mel Bay's Learn To Play Bluegrass Mandolin

Bud Orr
©1980 • Mel Bay Publications
**Type:** Songbook
**Level:** Beginner
**Number of Pages:** 48
**Notation:** Standard/Tablature

A thorough compilation of bluegrass and folk songs that introduce many basic techniques for the beginner to build on.

### VI. Mel Bay's Deluxe Country Mandolin Method

Bud Orr
©1980 • Mel Bay Publications
**Type:** Songbook
**Level:** Beginner
**Number of Pages:** 96
**Notation:** Standard/Tablature

A variety of folk, bluegrass and country tunes are offered. Excellent instruction for the rank beginner.

### VII. Bluegrass Mandolin

Jack Tottle
©1975 • Oak Publications
**Type:** Songbook & Methodology
**Level:** Beginner/Intermediate/Advanced
**Number of Pages:** 160
**Notation:** Standard/Tablature

A comprehensive book on learning how to play bluegrass mandolin. Excellent historical notes on bluegrass mandolin players are included. Includes a section on crosspicking mandolin with advanced arrangements.

### VIII. Mel Bay Presents Bluegrass Mandolin Techniques

Jethro Burns & Ken Eidson
©1982 • Mel Bay Publications
**Type:** Songbook
**Level:** Beginner/Intermediate/Advanced
**Number of Pages:** 80
**Notation:** Standard/Tablature

Jethro Burns' knowledge of chords is very evident with this work. To avoid playing the same positions over and over, as do many bluegrass mandolinists, try applying some of the possibilities explained by Jethro and Ken. These examples will add a lot of color to your backup and lead playing within a bluegrass context.

### IX. Mel Bay's Mandolin Songbook

Ken Eidson
©1980 • Mel Bay Publications
**Type:** Songbook
**Level:** Beginner
**Number of Pages:** 73
**Notation:** Standard/Tablature

Mostly consists of traditional folk songs. Includes bare-bones melody and many lyrics. Great for building your repertoire of folk favorites.

### X. Mandolin Instruction

Michael I. Holmes
©1977 • Folkways Records & Service Corp.
**Type:** Songbook
**Level:** Beginner/Intermediate
**Number of Pages:** 44
**Notation:** Tablature

A songbook consisting of basic arrangements of traditional fiddle tunes. Includes informative notes on buying a mandolin.

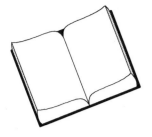

# A Selection for Further Study

## BLUEGRASS & FOLK INSTRUCTION (cont.)

### XI. Bluegrass Masters: Jesse McReynolds Mandolin

Andy Statman
©1979 • Oak Publications
**Type:** Songbook & Methodology
**Level:** Advanced
**Number of Pages:** 80
**Notation:** Tablature

A great collection of crosspicking tunes arranged by the master artist (Jesse McReynolds) who introduced crosspicking mandolin in the 1950s.

### XII. Mel Bay's Deluxe Bluegrass Mandolin Method

Ray Valla
©1974 • Mel Bay Publications
**Type:** Songbook
**Level:** Intermediate/Advanced
**Number of Pages:** 56
**Notation:** Standard/Tablature

The best reference source for building a repertoire of mandolin fiddle tunes. An accompanying recording is available to familiarize yourself to the tunes before attempting to learn them. Learn and memorize every tune in this book to build technique and be truly capable of playing in any bluegrass jam session.

### XIII. Teach Yourself Bluegrass Mandolin

Andy Statman
©1978 • Amsco Music Publishing Company
**Type:** Songbook
**Level:** Beginner/Intermediate
**Number of Pages:** 64
**Notation:** Standard/Tablature

Basic arrangements of many bluegrass standards are included. Of noted interest is the section on crosspicking which includes nice crosspicking arrangements of "Boil Them Cabbage Down" and "Swing Low".

### XIV. Mel Bay's Anthology of Mandolin Music

Bud Orr
©1983 • Mel Bay Publications
**Type:** Songbook
**Level:** Beginner/Intermediate/Advanced
**Number of Pages:** 224
**Notation:** Standard/Tablature

A diverse collection of mandolin arrangements that cover every genre, including bluegrass and folk—this book is a must-have if you're a performing mandolinist since many oft-requested tunes are included.

# A Selection for Further Study

## JAZZ & RAGTIME INSTRUCTION

### I. The Tiny Moore Mandolin Method

Tiny Moore
©1982 • Charles Anderson Music Publishing
**Type:** Songbook
**Level:** Advanced
**Number of Pages:** 48
**Notation:** Standard/Tablature

A selection of tunes arranged by Tiny Moore that are swing/ragtime oriented. Includes a great section on scales and arpeggios.

### II. Mal Bay Presents Jethro Burns Mandolin Picking Solos

Jethro Burns & Ken Eidson
©1980 • Mel Bay Publications
**Type:** Songbook
**Level:** Intermediate/Advanced
**Number of Pages:** 96
**Notation:** Standard/Tablature

Includes many traditional tunes (folk/bluegrass) arranged by the legendary Jethro Burns. An important feature are the many examples of chord melody technique and how it applies to these traditional tunes which is a standard jazz approach.

### III. Mel Bay Presents Jethro Burns Mandolin

Jethro Burns & Ken Eidson
©1976 • Mel Bay Publications
**Type:** Songbook
**Level:** Intermediate/Advanced
**Number of Pages:** 96
**Notation:** Standard/Tablature

Jethro Burns' arrangements of many traditional tunes (folk/bluegrass with jazz overtones. Has many exercises transcribed that are true fingerbusters. Includes chord diagrams of many possible inversions.

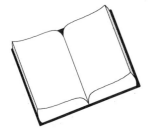

# A Selection for Further Study

## Fiddle Tune Collections

### I. Mel Bay Presents Ryan's Mammoth

Patrick Sky
©1995 • Mel Bay Publications
**Type:** Songbook
**Level:** Intermediate/Advanced
**Number of Pages:** 176
**Notation:** Standard

1050 reels, jigs, hornpipes, clogs, walk-arounds, essences, strathspeys, highland flings and contra dances offering a wealth of material for the mandolin player who can read standard notation. Originally published in 1883.

### II. O'Nell's Music of Ireland

Miles Krassen
©1976 • Oak Publications
**Type:** Songbook
**Level:** Intermediate/Advanced
**Number of Pages:** 254
**Notation:** Standard

Over 1000 Irish fiddle tunes offering an endless resource of jigs, reels, hornpipes, long dances and marches. Includes an introduction on the history of Irish Music.

### III. Mel Bay Presents The Phillips Collection of Traditional American Fiddle Tunes Volume One

Stacy Phillips
©1994 • Mel Bay Publications
**Type:** Songbook
**Level:** Intermediate/Advanced
**Number of Pages:** 391
**Notation:** Standard

A vast collection of hoedowns, breakdowns and reels exemplifying "what fiddlers in the United States are playing and listening to in the latter part of the twentieth century".

### IV. Mel Bay Presents The Phillips Collection of Traditional American Fiddle Tunes Volume Two

Stacy Phillips
©1995 • Mel Bay Publications
**Type:** Songbook
**Level:** Intermediate/Advanced
**Number of Pages:** 267
**Notation:** Standard

A continuation of the first volume with rags, blues, hornpipes, waltzes, polkas, and jigs. Of noted interest are the many interpretations presented by twentieth century fiddlers—consistent with the first volume. Both volumes offer a mandolinist many years of study and reference.

# A Selection for Further Study

## CLASSICAL MANDOLIN INSTRUCTION

### I. Mel Bay's Complete Mandolin Method

Mel Bay
©1968 • Mel Bay Publications
**Type:** Songbook/Methodology
**Level:** Beginner/Intermediate
**Number of Pages:** 96
**Notation:** Standard

A great introduction to reading music—methodical and cumulative in its approach to learning notes and timing. Includes many scale studies, etudes, duets, and solos that are based on previous exercises and studies.

### II. A Variety of Mandolin Music

Intro by Hugo d'Alton
©1975 • Clifford Essex Publications
**Type:** Songbook
**Level:** Advanced
**Number of Pages:** 40
**Notation:** Standard

A collection of late Victorian pieces all written in standard notation.

### III. The William Place Jr. Mandolin Method in Three Volumes

William Place, Jr.
©1934 • Mills Music
**Type:** Songbook/Methodology
**Level:** Beginner/Intermediate/Advanced
**Number of Pages:** Each Volume: 64
**Notation:** Standard

A great series for learning how to read standard notation for the mandolin. Includes many studies and traditional classical mandolin pieces that start from the first position and progressively end up on the seventh position.

### IV. Cristofaro A Method For Mandolin

F. de Cristofaro
©1975 • California Music Press
**Type:** Songbook/Methodology
**Level:** Intermediate/Advanced
**Number of Pages:** 80
**Notation:** Standard

Covers rudimentary note-reading through exercises and scales—advances too quickly for the complete beginner. Of noted interest is the thorough section on scale intervals.

### V. The Bickford Mandolin Method In Two Volumes

Zarh Myron Bickford
©1920 • Carl Fischer
**Type:** Songbook/Methodology
**Level:** Beginner/Intermediate/Advanced
**Number of Pages:** Total: 175
**Notation:** Standard

The music reflects the period in which it was written—a thorough treatise on how to read standard notation. All of the pieces are written in duet format. Loads of fun if you can find another mandolinist to play the harmony parts.

# Resources

An extensive selection of new & used instruments, recordings, instructional material and instrument accessories is offered by Elderly Instruments in Lansing, Michigan.
Write or call for further info:
**Elderly Instruments**
1100 N. Washington
PO Box 14210
Lansing, MI 48901
(517) 372-7890
Web address at: http://www.elderly.com


Many contemporary mandolin recordings are offered by Acoustic Disc. Write or call for their most recent newsletter/catalog:
**Acoustic Disc**
PO Box 4143
San Rafael, CA 94913
(415) 545-1187
Web address at: http://www.dawgnet.com


The Mel Bay Complete Catalog is the ultimate resource for instruction material that covers all instruments in all genres.
**Mel Bay Publications, Inc.**
#4 Industrial Drive
Pacific, MO 63069-0066
1-800-8-MEL BAY
Web address at: http://www.melbay.com


PHOTO CREDITS:
Steve Szilagyi
Dave Matchette